Teaching Our Story

Teaching
Our
Story

Narrative Leadership
and Pastoral Formation

~

Larry A. Golemon, Editor

THE
ALBAN
INSTITUTE
Herndon, Virginia
www.alban.org

The Alban Institute
2121 Cooperative Way, Suite 100
Herndon, VA 20171

Scripture quotations, unless otherwise noted, are from the New Revised Standard Version of the Bible, copyright © 1989, Division of Christian Education of the National Council of Churches of Christ in the United States of America, and are used by permission.

Cover design by Spark Design.

Library of Congress Cataloging-in-Publication Data

Teaching our story : narrative leadership and pastoral formation / Larry A. Golemon, editor.
    p. cm.
  Includes bibliographical references.
  ISBN 978-1-56699-377-7
  1. Storytelling--Religious aspects--Christianity. 2. Narrative theology. 3. Christian leadership. 4. Pastoral theology. I. Golemon, Larry A.
  BT83.78.T43 2009
  230'.046--dc22
                        2009038345

10   11   12   13   14   VP   5   4   3   2   1

Contents

~

Preface

~

Teachers and students of theological education have long wrestled with ways to integrate the competing demands of academics, spiritual formation, and professional education in seminaries. These same demands still impinge on pastors once in ministry. This volume explores one set of strategies—around narrative practices—that helps build bridges between theological disciplines and the various practices of ministry. These essays grew out of conversations with theological educators and pastors in the Alban Institute's Narrative Leadership Project, graciously supported by the Luce Foundation.

Narrative approaches to integrating theological learning and ministry are not new. Students and teachers in theological education have explored various ways to integrate the fields of seminary education, many of which have included narrative dimensions. In the nineteenth century, most seminaries taught rhetoric and elocution as the capstone of their curricula, toward the goal of producing public orators. In the twentieth century, various integrating strategies were employed, ranging from historical methods to progressive education's emphasis on social practice to reigning theologies of neo-orthodoxy or neo-Thomism. Each of these approaches often assumed a master narrative as the cohesive factor in learning. A lasting solution proved elusive, though, as the research and teaching methods, curricular struggles, and guilds of the various disciplines resisted integration into a larger paradigm. So, many educators and students began to embrace strategies of teaching and learning that seemed to cut across the disciplines—including contextual analysis and praxis, methods of spiritual formation, gender and culture studies, and narrative interpretation.

This volume celebrates new narrative approaches to integrating teaching and learning in theological education and the practice of ministry. Narrative studies have helped revitalize various fields of study in recent years and, we at Alban believe, are some of the most promising teaching strategies that help sustain ministry practices over time. In this volume, readers will hear from a biblical scholar, a practical theologian, a homiletician, a systematic theologian, a campus pastor and educator, and a postseminary educator about how narrative methods have enlivened their disciplines and their teaching and learning around ministry. The book emphasizes how various teachers use narrative methods to help integrate classroom, contextual, and continuing education with unusual creativity. While many of the essays are told from the point of view of teaching and learning, each one of them relates directly to practices and challenges of contemporary ministry, which will benefit any pastor or lay minister. Teachers and ongoing students of theology will find promising narrative approaches to the learning and practice of theology that will enhance their own ministries.

In the first essay, I share a framework for integrating narrative approaches that helps inform theological education and ministry practice. As the director of the Narrative Leadership project at the Alban Institute for several years, I identify five principles that arose from the Alban research into narrative studies from various fields of practice. I distill basic insights from Dan McAdams' psychological research on the redemptive self, Jerome Bruner's use of narrative and culture in education theory, and Howard Gardner's study of narrative in public leadership to find basic principles that promote personal generativity, the construction of meaning, and the process of change in ministry. I also draw upon Diana Butler Bass's work in church practices to argue that narratives are closely related to religious practices and tradition in generating and sustaining congregational vitality. In the end, this essay offers five principles or practical norms that will help any teacher or minister reflect more effectively on their own use of narrative approaches to their work.

In the second essay, Judy Fentress-Williams offers a paradigm of dialogical narrative for reading Deuteronomy and the story of Ruth. As professor of Hebrew Scripture at Virginia Theological Seminary, Fentress-Williams offers an approach to reading scripture that opens traditional narrative approaches—which seek an official reading—to the multiple voices and perspectives in a text. By drawing on her own work with the Russian critic Mikhael Bakhtin, she explores how the command to remember in Deuteronomy is a textual strategy that resists forgetting or glossing over a painful history, like wandering in the wilderness. Then she explores how narrative strategies in the book of Ruth negotiate a shift in identity for the foreigner Ruth, other women like Naomi, and the people of Israel. By negotiating a new covenant, free from cultural norms of attachment to men or nationality, both Ruth and Naomi rewrite the meaning of faithfulness, personhood, and nation. This opening of one's culture and national identity to new voices and narrative negotiation has profound implications for ministry in a contemporary America populated by "foreigners."

Susan Hedahl, in the third chapter, explores the implications of shared scriptural narratives in the divergent homiletical traditions of Christianity, Judaism, and Islam. She offers a rich case study of a course in interreligious comparative homiletics that she teaches at Gettysburg Theological Seminary. She brings her background in rhetorical studies and communication to the course objectives, strategies, and evaluation—all of which are built around studying specific sermons and preaching practices from each tradition. Students explore the logos of these sermons by focusing on the shared narrative core of the stories of Abraham, where they are quickly thrown into comparative scriptural studies of the Bible and the Qur'an and comparative study of sermons from one faith tradition placed alongside those of the others. They also explore a classic understanding of ethos in the preacher's character as a religious leader, and the rhetorical strategies such leaders use to admonish, persuade, teach, and warn. Finally, they explore the pathos of how these sermons speak to the communities they are set in. In the end, Hedahl raises important questions about how such a course speaks to preaching in the interreligious context of contemporary America.

In the fourth chapter, Mary Moschella explores how the study of local narratives of faith communities builds more effective pastoral leaders. As professor of pastoral theology at Wesley Seminary, Moschella shares her pioneering work in "pastoral ethnography," which she describes as "a practice than can enliven the stories people and congregations tell and open the way for creative improvisation as a community composes the future chapters of its shared life." She draws on the multiple disciplines of sociology, congregational studies, and practical theology to explore the unique form that ethnographic practices, like interviews and participant observation, can take when used in pastoral leadership, in contrast to a transient researcher. Through these practices, pastors learn how to listen to the multiple cultural and social narratives of a local congregation, identify their own hopes for the community in the research process, and from this dialogue shape a more viable story and theology for their shared future. Moschella shares moving examples from her own teaching and students' research that explore the methodology, ethics, theological discernment, and leadership decisions required for effective pastoral ethnography to be put into practice. She also reflects on the powerful impact such congregational-based studies have on the formation of future religious leaders.

Kathryn Vitalis Hoffman describes how the art of story brokering is taught in contextual or field education at Gettysburg Theological Seminary. She offers a case study of a course that placed eight students in neighborhood settings—from coffee shops to exercise classes to local foodbanks—as places for intentional pastoral conversations to emerge. Hoffman builds on methods of narrative research to describe a process of ministerial story brokering that involves careful attending, evoking, and listening to people's lives and stories, interlacing their stories with biblical narratives, and discerning and sharing an emerging story. She describes how narrative inquiry is used in various teaching strategies of the course—from cohort groups to online conversations and analysis of a congregation in light of postmodern stories. She shares students' experiences of overcoming snap impressions by learning to thicken people's stories, learning not to be defensive about organized religion, and learning to faithfully represent others' stories in class presentations and preaching. Finally, students are invited to weave some of these stories, and those from other parts of their lives, with biblical narratives to open up redemptive and transformative possibilities. Hoffman closes with reflections on how this learning experience shaped the ministerial identity of students and the wider seminary community.

Robert Anderson, an experienced pastor and interim ministry educator, shares his reflections on the narrative shape of "redemptive leadership" in the sixth chapter. He begins with an autobiographical reflection on how the themes of hope and redemption emerged in his own childhood. He reflects on how his call to interim ministry and his approach to teaching continuing education in ministry at Pittsburgh Theological Seminary is shaped by narratives of hope and redemption. He teaches four distinct narrative practices to interims and other ministers in transition situations. The first involves identifying the soul of a congregation by tracing its story of mission and purpose. The second is practicing pastoral presence by sharing one's own life story with care and being open to how a congregation will add to one's story. The third is a deep or soulful listening, which allows silences to help people reframe their story. The fourth and fifth practices involve the story-weaving of a community's many tales, and working with the community to build a new story. Finally, the sixth practice is the art of future storying, which builds a shared, viable story for the future. Throughout, Anderson shares personal narratives, congregational accounts, and theological insights that will help any educator or pastor reflect on the way redemptive stories shape their own practice.

The book ends with a fitting piece of local narrative theology by Susan Kendall, director of the Doctor of Ministry Program at Pittsburgh Theological Seminary. She demonstrates how the artful weaving of stories of place with an eye to opportunities amidst change helps shape a place-based theology of ministry for a postmodern age. In short, Kendall offers a theological poetic on her own place of ministry—the city of Pittsburgh—by reflecting on towering, abandoned churches, boarded-up steel mills, hillside terrains now veiled by factory smoke, the shifting dreams of immigrants, and the new opportunities for work and neighborhood. Instead of letting cultural and social change overrun cherished beliefs—as happened for Rome and the Enlightenment—she calls on pastoral leaders and theologians to attend to the ongoing process of change, the multitude of voices in local culture, and the cracks that begin to appear in any fixed narrative of place "so that we as leaders are able to cultivate and claim agency in the midst of change for the sake of the gospel." She challenges religious and civic leaders to resist turning narratives of change or loss over to tragedy or nostalgia by watching for that which is redeemable and renewing in conditions of abrupt change. Learning to live in the disorientation and displacement that change can bring to one's sense of rootedness creates the luminal space for new narratives of hope—including those about faith and tradition—to emerge.

In the end, these gifted educators and ministers offer a range of narrative approaches to theological studies and the practice ministry that will enrich conversations in the academy, the local church, and denominational programs of life-long learning. I commend each of them to you, as you learn ways to re-story the faith for your own community and your vocation.

Larry A. Golemon
Director
The Alban Institute Narrative Leadership Project

CHAPTER I

Toward a Framework for Narrative Leadership in Ministry

⌒

LARRY A. GOLEMON

Ministry in the biblical traditions has utilized stories of faith for identity and renewal since the beginning. Jews celebrate the founding story of the exodus in their homes each Sabbath, and their tradition is laced with rabbinical midrash. Early Christians put the life, death, and resurrection of Jesus into the story forms of preaching, liturgy, and a unique genre called the Gospels. Narrative forms and storytelling are so much a part of Jewish and Christian practice, in fact, that most congregations take them for granted.

While stories of faith are second nature to local congregations, American popular culture has learned to exploit them in powerful ways. Bluegrass, gospel, country, and even hip-hop render images and stories of faith in new musical idioms. Hollywood and Broadway have capitalized on stories of faith in modern classics like *The Bells of St. Mary's* (1945) and *Fiddler on the Roof* (1964), and television has captured the faith craze in hit series like *Touched by an Angel* (1994–2003). Public tragedies bring an outpouring of popular sentiment laced with religion—as in the death of Princess Diana in 1997 or the aftermath of 9/11. Yet, while popular culture and practice recognize the power of faith stories to address modern life, many churches and synagogues have yet to recognize the potential of their own narrative work for revitalizing religious traditions and practices.

At the Alban Institute, we believe the time has come to lift up the power of these narrative traditions and the art of story crafting and performance as primary resources for congregational leadership and renewal. For the past two years, the Alban Institute has been engaged in a research project called the Narrative Leadership project, made possible by the Luce Foundation, which involved pastors, lay leaders, seminary educators, and some congregations in an exploration of the narrative resources and activities of ministry. We have tapped the growing expertise of Alban consultants in narrative theory and practice. Through it all, the power of storytelling and narrative approaches to leadership have convinced us that this is a groundbreaking arena for developing new forms of pastoral and lay leadership in ministry. In short, we believe good narrative leadership has the potential to transform congregational traditions, practices, and mission for the current age.

The Narrative Situation

The playwright Paul Auster wrote, "Stories happen to people who are able to tell them."[1] Otherwise, stuff and crises "happen" to them. People who learn to shape life experiences into narrative form find patterns of meaning and response open to them. People who can reframe life events—especially those of hardship and tragedy—into stories of resilience, discovery, and growth can shape a life narrative that funds personal agency, faithfulness, and civic responsibility.

The prospects of building coherent, life-giving narratives in this day and age, however, are highly debated. Postmodern theorists of contemporary society, like Jean-Francois Lyotard, argue that the "master narratives" that shaped modern, Enlightenment society—for example, the reflective self, historical progress, universal reason, and the enlightenment of science— have eroded or collapsed.[2] Parallel changes in religion—like the decline of biblical literacy, authority, and confessional traditions—confirm that the grand narratives of denominations and congregational life no longer hold the power they once did.

Because larger framing narratives are missing, people are bombarded by an endless stream of images, vignettes, and emotional moments in this media-driven culture, to the point that many become experiential receptacles, or what psychologist Kenneth Gergen calls "saturated selves."[3] Others learn to roleplay several identities—one at home, one at work, one while traveling—in a postmodern pastiche that often exhausts moral energy and focus.

As master narratives of religious tradition and modernity decline, new forms of narrative construction arise to fill the void. The moral philosopher Charles Taylor describes how self-narration arose in the modern period to replace or reconstruct older, inherited schemes: "[One] can only find an identity in self-narration. Life has to be lived as a story. . . . But now it becomes harder to take over the story ready-made from the canonical models and archetypes" of religious tradition or Enlightenment.[4] To form a rich, personal, and life-giving narrative, one must construct a sense of spatial location in the world from which direction and agency can spring. This happens only by mapping that world through story.

Two of the narrative "sources of the self" that Taylor identifies appear to be at odds with each other in the American context. The Romantic tradition—through writers like Emerson, landscape painting, and the modern novel—elevates "expressive individualism" as the primary form of self-narration. This form of personal narrative seeps into popular culture through the lone hero in film (like Rambo or Jason Bourne), the self-realization movement in pop psychology, and new age spirituality. The communitarian tradition elevates social practices and belonging—through traditional religion, ethnic community, generational affinity, or nationalism—as the primary locus of identity. The explosion of virtual communities in online chatrooms, Facebook, blogs, and Twitter is an attempt to build new, nonspatial communities as a place to construct one's own story.

A new focus on the narrative leadership and the narrative work of ministry can develop congregations as a primary source for *place-forming* narratives in American society. Lifting up congregations as story-formed and forming communities draws upon the strength of communitarianism to locate personal identity within a given community. Lifting up the power of personal narratives to reshape congregational traditions and practice draws upon the strength of individualism to link moral agency and meaning with living narratives of one's own making. In short, we believe the time has come for a *community-based individualism* in American religious life—one made possible by a new emphasis on the power of story in local congregations.

Narrative leadership in American churches and synagogues has the potential to transform personal lives, congregational practice and mission, and even the wider social fabric. If a person's location in the world can be mapped in and through congregational life, then his or her sense of moral agency to make a difference in that world can be enhanced. If congregations can encourage community-based individualism among their members, their personal stories will be entwined with that primary community and they will learn a form of story linking that can extend to other areas of their life: from family to work to civic engagement. As Christian and Jewish congregations become intentional story-forming communities, they can shape the lives of millions of Americans as generative, faithful, and civic-minded adults.

Narrative Frameworks in Theological Education

~

The use of narrative theory and practices has been part of theological scholarship for some time. Scholars like Hans Frei, Paul Ricoeur, Stanley Hauerwas, and Mary Doak have developed different approaches to narrative theology.[5] Biblical scholars like Brevard Childs, Walter Brueggemann, Richard Hays, and Gail O'Day have adopted different narrative strategies, often under the rubrics of canonical, rhetorical, intertextual, or narrative criticism.[6] The narrative therapy movement, developed by Michael White and David Epston, has influenced pastoral care and counseling through Christie Neugar and others.[7] Narrative approaches to homiletics by Eugene Lowry, Fred Craddock, and others have made a significant impact.[8] Narrative hermeneutics has influenced the liturgical theology of David Power, Joyce Zimmerman, and others as well.[9] James Hopewell redefined congregational studies by his use of narrative analysis,[10] which spawned a new emphasis on local narratives in that field.[11] The church practices movement is beginning to see the power of narratives to revitalize and sustain Christian practices over time.[12] While the impact on retrieving religious tradition through narrative frameworks has been profound, to date these theories have not been woven together into a coherent framework for ministry and congregational renewal.

Religious leaders can harness the power of narratives—in religious tradition and people's lives—to develop a new understanding of ministry and leadership that can change the face of American congregations. By cultivating local churches and synagogues as story-formed and forming communities, narrative leaders can transform the traditions and practices of the religious congregations they serve. To do so, we believe developing a framework that relates narrative work to the full range of congregational life is important.

Narrative, Religious Tradition, and Practices in Congregational Life

~

During Alban's Narrative Leadership project, we have discovered that the narrative work of pastors, lay leaders, and congregations is multifaceted and complex. By *narrative work* we mean the intentional retrieval, construction, and performance of narratives in all arenas of ministry and congregational life. Narrative work does not stand on its own, but relates closely to the inherited traditions and cultivated practices of each church or synagogue. It takes place in all arenas of congregational life: worship, pastoral care and small groups, religious education and governance, formal governance and informal networks, and much more. By relating narrative leadership more closely to current work on religious tradition and practices, we have found that religious traditions, narratives, and practices fund each other in a dynamic, generative relationship.

Good narrative work revitalizes tradition by generating practices that reembody that tradition for a new place and time. By *tradition* we mean the scriptural, liturgical, moral, and theological norms and customs that are passed down from generation to generation in a self-conscious way. Tradition grows out of the tacit knowledge or habitus of a way of life,[13] but gradually it becomes self-conscious as "an historically extended, socially embodied argument . . . about the goods which constitute that tradition."[14] In Christianity and Judaism, self-conscious traditions are often sustained by text-based arguments about what norms, beliefs, and customs of the Bible, Talmud, and ritual or theological texts are recognized as quintessential to the tradition.

Religious practices, according to Diana Butler Bass, are things that congregations "do together in community that form them in God's love for the world."[15] Practices in this sense are forms of social interaction that extend the values or goods of the practice to higher levels of excellence and to more participants, in ways that form them for service to and with God. The more intentional leaders are about the way they retrieve, construct, and present narratives, the more tradition and social practices transform each other. We believe the narrative work of congregations—through sustained retrieval, construction, and presentation of the stories of faith—lies at the heart of a renewing relationship between tradition and social practices. As Diana Butler Bass writes, "Tradition is embodied in practices. And practices convey meaning through narrative."[16] This dynamic, mutually supporting relationship between tradition, narratives, and practices can be illustrated as a circle of generativity:

Narratives

Tradition   Practices

At the center of this generative circle lies the imagination as the key human capacity that moves from tradition through narratives and practices and back again. Both the pastoral imagination and the congregational imagination are exercised and deepened as religious traditions are revitalized through narratives and renewed practices.[17] As Diana Butler Bass puts it, "Imagination is the stage on which narrative, tradition, and practice perform their dance."[18] As the imagination discerns what is most valued by the community in each of these movements and intentionally shapes them according to these identified norms, it becomes a deeper theological imagination. Theological discernment and intention are not part of a separate moment in this circle, but are integral to all three movements.

Drawing on Contemporary Narrative Research

We have come to understand that a compelling framework for narrative ministry must broaden the conversation beyond theological studies. To identify the transformative characteristics of narratives, the social process of narrative construction, and features of narrative leadership, we have drawn on three narrative researchers from psychology, education, and leadership development: Dan McAdams, psychologist at Northwestern University; Jerome Bruner, education theorist at New York University; and Howard Gardner, psychologist and leadership theorist. Each one makes a distinctive contribution to what transformative, life-giving narratives look like and to the role of communities and their leaders in building narrative-rich congregations.

McAdams and the Redemptive Self

Contemporary research in life narratives confirms the resilience and creativity of people to construct stories of meaning and identity, even when grand narratives of religion and Enlightenment are collapsing. In *The Redemptive Self: Stories Americans Live By*, psychologist Dan McAdams describes the power of redemptive narratives in the lives of hundreds of generative adults he has interviewed.[19] By drawing on Erik Erikson's view of the "generative adult,"[20] McAdams identifies the features of adults who "pass on to posterity" a feature of themselves for the benefit of future generations.[21] In short, they make their mark on others through a range of cultural activities—from childrearing, to work production, to volunteering, and to religious or political activity. Through surveys and interviews, McAdams identified six features of the personal narratives of generative adults, which appeared over and over again:

> *Childhood advantage*: strong family, school achievement, status in organization or a special talent, appearance, or a stroke of luck;
> *Awareness of the suffering of others*: due to a family loss, social tragedy, or exposure to suffering in one's community;
> *Moral depth and steadfastness*: strong belief system, religious upbringing, or moral education that stays through life;
> *Redemption*: tragedy, hardship, or bad luck are seen as producing positive outcomes;
> *Power versus love*: needs for influence and power often conflict with needs for intimacy and love;
> *Future growth*: anticipation, even optimism, that the things and people they have cared about and generated will flourish in the future. [22]

The fourth feature of generative adults, redemption, is of special interest to McAdams. What marks someone's story as redemptive is the person's ability to reframe tragedy or suffering in terms of opportunity, positive change, or growth. McAdams found six genres of redemptive life story, each of which is tied to a tradition of American storytelling: (a) atonement stories that are rooted in religious narratives; (b) emancipation stories, rooted in political narratives of freedom; (c) upward mobility stories rooted in economic stories of the "self-made man;" (d) recovery stories rooted in medical and therapeutic narratives; (e) enlightenment stories rooted in educational and scientific narratives; and (f) development stories rooted in narratives of psychology and parenting. McAdams's work is remarkable because it illustrates the direct link between personal narratives, life fulfillment, and social productivity—even in the midst of decaying master narratives. In other words, people remain resilient in their story-forming and storytelling ability, even when society forgets how.

The implications of McAdams's research for the narrative work of ministry are far-reaching. The first three features of generative life stories—advantage, suffering of others, and moral depth—outline a virtual curriculum for early childhood and family nurture in congregations. Storytelling, liturgies, and mission experiences for children and families can instill empathy for others' hardship, moral capacities and clarity, and a sense of specialness as one of God's children and servants. Establishing venues for adults to share their own stories of tragedy and listen to others'—through small groups, prayer partners, and lay visitation programs—allows members to reframe hardships as opportunities for change and growth, and is essential. Providing a framework of the future through stories of hope—like passing on the faith from generation to generation or by painting a promise-filled eschatology—can enhance personal stories of optimism and confidence. Above all, McAdams's focus on the redemptive self invites churches and synagogues to mine their own traditions for stories of atonement or emancipation, of hard work or healing, of enlightenment or growth in ways that make these genres of redemptive change commonplace and accessible to people so that they may integrate and adapt them to their own life narratives.

Bruner and the Narrative Construction of Meaning

Jerome Bruner, noted cultural psychologist and educator, identifies narrative cognition as one of the primary modes of knowing.[23] In contrast to *logical-scientific* language used for objects and causation, *narrative* language focuses on the world of agency and intent—including that of self and others. Bruner sets out to remedy the West's preoccupation with scientific knowledge by convincing others that "narrative understanding is crucial to constructing our lives and a 'place' for ourselves in the possible world we will encounter."[24] For our purposes, I will focus on the four aspects of the narrative construction of meaning he has identified that inform how religious communities can shape their narratives: a distinct view of time, a focus on human intention, the importance of choice of genre, and the regular disruption of canons.

Narratives create a distinct understanding of *time*, claims Bruner, that is quite different from the chronological time of science. By drawing on the work of philosopher Paul Ricoeur, Bruner claims that stories construct a sense of "humanly relevant time" that focuses on meaning-making and agency.[25] Folk tales, myths, novels, and even the Bible use temporal strategies like foreshadowing, flashbacks, anamnesis, or prolepsis in order to relate crucial events to the decisions and interpretations given to them in story form. By extension, people learn to do the same in their own lives—by recalling certain events as foreshadowing a present tragedy or by seeing in a young child's choice of drawing or building as the proleptic anticipation of a future career. Even larger units of time—like epochs, dynasties, or centuries—frame the story of smaller events by relating them to the meaning of the whole: the Bronze Age, the Han Dynasty, or the Age of Reason. The Bible is especially fond of placing human events and epochs within the larger temporal horizon of divine providence and action. Religious narratives often suspend our own sense of relevance within a more complex, if not mysterious, causal nexus of God's purpose.

Related to human relevance, narratives are shaped by the *intentions* of human agency by multiple players, not by the laws of causation or explanation from science. Bruner writes, "Some element of freedom is always implied in narrative," which often intrudes upon a "presumed causal chain" like fate or destiny.[26] Stories are shaped by what he calls the "intentional states" of beliefs, desires, theories, and values of their actors, which often test, cajole, or even overturn wider causal networks at hand. In the Homeric myths, for example, only Ulysses' cunning saves him from the hands of fate. In the Bible, only Abraham's plead-ing with God can save Sodom (Gen. 18). Narratives hold our interest and inform our lives to the extent they make a case for human agency and interests. Because narratives employ a variety of actors and their reasons for things, their meanings are always intersubjective and negotiable. Narrative work, at its best, is socially interactive through debate, competition, and collaboration.

What *genre* people choose to frame a story, however, is criti-cal. Genres—like comedy, tragedy, irony, and romance—not only arrange certain events and actions, but these particular genres also become "tokens of more inclusive types."[27] Which genre we choose to fashion an experience into story determines the events, actions, and characters we will highlight and what their range of functions can be. In short, genre choice deter-mines how the parts are related to the whole in a framework of interpretation. The figure of Socrates, for example, was por-trayed as a tragic hero in Plato's dialogues, but then as a comic farce in Aristophanes' play, *The Clouds*. James Hopewell, one of the founders of congregational studies, claimed that congrega-tions got stuck in certain mythic forms or genres and had to learn to reframe their experiences in more redemptive forms.[28] Whether a congregational loss or conflict is portrayed as an inevitable tragedy or as an ironic moment of opportunity, for example, makes all the difference.

Part of the longevity and power of narratives lies in their ability to disrupt and reframe inherited *canons* of meaning from tradition. Bruner writes of the innovative storyteller as "a powerful cultural figure provided his [or her] stories take off from conventional narrative canons and lead to our seeing what had never before been 'noticed.'"[29] As Bruner states, a new story plays off of established canons of meaning and value as it "tempts new genres into being." Shakespeare reworks tragic legends like Lear and historical accounts like Richard III to create something entirely new. So, too, the New Testament plays off of figures and types in the Hebrew Scriptures—from Adam to Moses to Isaiah—to create a new vision of God's redemptive work. Both Jewish and Christian canons are filled with stories of disrupting traditions: from the cunning of Jacob that steals a birthright to the parabolic challenges of Jesus to established rules and hierarchies. Bruner summarizes by saying effective narratives trade on the "centrality of trouble," because they are constantly overturning the canonical apple cart.[30]

Taken together, these four features of narrative work—*time, intentions, genre, and canon*—emphasize the fluid, negotiable, and ever-changing dynamics of narrative construction and extension. While narrative work can begin at very local, even domesticated levels, the dynamics of their development and their ability to extend to wider levels of narrative engagement—including Scripture and sacred history itself, means that narrative work is an ongoing and necessary part of religious leadership. While Bruner addresses the major characteristics of narrative work, hints about how leaders harness the power of narratives for creating new social realities must be found elsewhere.

Gardner on Narrative Leadership in Public Life

Howard Gardner, noted theorist in education and leadership, has documented the importance of narrative retrieval and construction in relation to public leadership.[31] Several of his findings have direct implications for the narrative work of congregations and their leaders, including the various kinds of stories and their developmental implications, the difference between storytelling in public versus specialized domains, and the characteristics of developed leaders and their narrative work.

Gardner identifies three kinds of stories in the narrative work of leaders, each with its own implications for human development. *Personal stories* engage the sense of self and its place in the world, often at very basic levels. Here, the "five-year-old mind" is presented as a primal, even mythic, world of good versus evil, of safety and danger that each person must negotiate throughout life. *Communal stories* engage group identity also at the basic level of the five-year-old mind—like "us" versus "them"—but then in increasingly sophisticated ways. Group belonging for the "ten-year-old mind," for example, is built upon a clear sense of rules and fair play. Finally, *evaluative stories* of what is good, beautiful, and true present the deepest values of a community and invite human subjects to embrace or adapt them. Normative stories largely go unquestioned by the five- and ten-year-old minds, but the "fifteen-year-old mind" engages them with critique and adaptation. Rich and complete narratives, like Greek myths or biblical tales, include all three kinds of story—personal, communal, and evaluative—and can speak to the different levels of the five-, ten-, and fifteen-year-old minds when interpreted well.

Leaders in *public domains* make different use of narratives than those in *specialized domains*, like the professions. Gardner describes how leaders in the public arenas of politics, the military, or religion, for example, deal with broad-based populations who have an "ordinary frame of mind" unaffected by any specialized knowledge they may have. Popular leaders, like Ronald Reagan, learn to speak to the common man or woman in everyone by drawing upon what is familiar and shared in popular experience. They appeal directly to their audiences, and they adapt existing worldviews to new situations rather than invent new paradigms. By contrast, leaders in specialized domains—like medicine, law, or an academic field—deal with audiences that have a "sophisticated mind" shaped by specialized knowledge and technical terms. These domains expect novelty, invention, and vision from their leaders' stories, not a reinforcement of the familiar. Leaders in these domains, like Francis Collins of the human genome, exercise indirect influence through creating new models, theories, or paradigms. Clergy and congregational leaders clearly walk between the roles of public and specialized domain leader, depending on the audience and the level of sophistication they are engaged with.

Finally, Gardner identifies the characteristics of *developed leaders* in ways that mark their narrative abilities. First, developed leaders must embody and communicate the dominant story they tell on a regular basis, and in ways that elicit other people's choice to embrace or adapt that story. In ministry, this means that effective ministry must include regular opportunities to tell one's own story so that others experience congruity between the pastor's person and the congregation's story. Second, developed leaders maintain close ties with their community and they engage in a regular rhythm of contact and reflection. This means regular contact through pastoral visitation, e-mails, phone calls, and hallway conversations is the business of good leadership, as it provides regular feedback and opportunity for reflection upon what people respond to. Third, developed leaders must combine symbolic-linguistic intelligence with personal intelligence as they engage their communities. Learning to exegete and reinterpret sacred texts and tradition is important for religious leaders, but so are the personal rapport, self-identification, and emotional honesty that are required to reach people with the resources of meaning.

In the end, Gardner's account of narrativity and leadership reminds us how complex the art of narrative work in congregational leadership can be. The need to work with an array of storytelling (personal, communal, and evaluative), the ability to shift between ordinary and sophisticated audiences in relation to faith issues, and the importance of embodying and sharing the story through regular contact and multiple intelligences are all vital for effective ministry. This review of Gardner completes my distillation of narrative theorists toward the aim of developing principles of narrative leadership in ministry.

Principles of Narrative Leadership in Ministry

~

The work of McAdams on personal narrative, Bruner on characteristics of narrative, and Gardner on narrative leadership suggest four key principles for narrative leadership in ministry.

Principle 1

Redemptive stories of faith place human meaning within the scope of divine time in order to form persons, communities, and their normative values.

Religious communities recast narratives from their traditions in ways that speak to human relevance and meaning in the present. Narratives retrieved from the Bible or Talmud usually do so by suspending human schemas of action and time in a wider matrix of divine purpose or mystery. Human time finds its place within divine time, often by recasting memories of saving events in the past, like the exodus, or through anticipating promises to be fulfilled, like the Messiah's coming or return. Even while relating human time to divine purpose, religious narratives usually do so in ways that form our sense of self, community, and the norms of beauty, goodness, and truth we live by. Forming a strong moral framework, informed by deep empathy with the suffering of others, is key. Narrative construction is more than retrieval, however, as it entails new negotiations of identity, belonging, and values for a community in its place and time. Finding redemptive themes or genres in

stories that people can adapt to their own lives is key: atonement, liberation, healing, illumination, or development are all
possibilities. Only narrative forms can capture this dynamic,
purposeful, yet relative sense of human agency and meaning
within something larger and more powerful.

Principle 2

*Narrative leaders in ministry use personal and symbolic intelli-
gence to draw their congregations into story retrieval, construction,
and response that are collaborative and intentional.*

Clergy and other congregational leaders draw upon emotional and symbolic intelligence as they invite others to engage
the narratives of their religious tradition. The ability to interpret
the texts and narratives of a tradition in ways that lift up redemptive themes for others is crucial, and doing so in ways that
invite others to participate in that interpretive act is a mark of
good narrative leadership. Good narrative retrieval, reconstruction, and response are most effective when done in collaborative ways through ongoing contact, reflection, and conversation
with the community. Only such collaborative action and shared
reflection can build the capacity to select and use stories in
intentional ways. In short, effective narrative leadership is a
collaborative action, which involves the community in story
selection, reconstruction, and negotiation over interpretations.
Communal methods of Bible study—like the African threefold
method,[32] base-group Bible study, or group *lectio divina*—can
build patterns of collaborative interpretation and reflection into
a congregation's life. The expertise of pastors may help identify
the richest and most relevant texts and stories, but unless the
community resonates with them and can rework them in their
own terms, they often fall flat. Narrative leaders invite their
communities to reflect upon stories that are provided or chosen,
often by retelling them with new insights and meanings. Effective leaders often guide from behind by providing insights from

their own discipline of reflection and prayer around how deep
the story work of the community is going.

Principle 3

*The choice of genre or redemptive motifs for a given story clarifies
how the details of character and plot relate to a broader purpose for
a faith community and what options of response are available to it.*

Public leaders are also sensitive to the dominant genre and
motifs of a story they develop to respond to a crisis or challenge. Whether a crisis is met with irony or tragedy sets in
place a range of facts, plotlines, and purposes that elicit certain
choices. American narratives after 9/11 were shaped by the heroic tragedy of a struggle between good and evil. But had they
been couched as irony, the contradictions between American
ideals of liberty and its global practices of exploitation might
have been reckoned with. How clergy and other congregational
leaders cast the stories of their community—as comic, tragic,
ironic, or romantic—will highlight certain facts and conceal
others as they are shaped into a wider pattern of meaning and
purpose. Congregational conflict is not always a tragic win-
lose; sometimes it is downright comic and restorative. Identifying the inherited genre and offering alternatives to it lift up
new facts and offer new choices previously blinded by a genre
choice. How leaders depict the future—as a tragic Armaged-
don or a comic restoration—will shape their appropriation of
key biblical texts. The way that suffering is framed—through
redemptive motifs of forgiveness, emancipation, healing, or enlightenment—will help people and communities shape their
own choices and responses to hardship in their lives. In specialized domains—of a profession, the sciences, or an academic
field—the choice of genre often shapes one's outcome: a failed
experiment may be a tragic loss of resources or a comedy of er-
rors, with many hidden learnings. In the sociology of religion,
mainline decline may be seen as a tragic inevitability or as an

ironic turn of fortune, which allows new patterns of congregational and denominational life to emerge.

Principle 4

Reconstructive narratives appeal to canonical understandings of tradition and practice, but they invite the canon's disruption and renegotiation as a sign of the tradition's vitality.
New narratives or narrative twists on old themes have the power to tweak, disrupt, and overturn established understandings and ways of doing things in congregations. This may be the most surprising feature of narrative leadership in congregations, as it challenges both traditionalism and progressivism. If traditions are revitalized chiefly through narrative work, as we at Alban claim, then there are no easy formulas—like "hold on to fundamentals" or "everything is getting better and better"—that have marked the divides in American religion in the past. How the sacraments or other rites are done, when children are confirmed, or how new members are welcomed can be transformed through new narrative frameworks. Most renovations and reformations of Christian and Jewish traditions have involved a return to past stories, but with a new narrative focus and poignancy that make them timely and transformative. Many generative adults stretch and adapt their childhood moral frameworks, rather than completely replace them, as a witness to both the resilience and flexibility of religious frameworks. The more confident congregations become in their own generativity into future generations, they more they are willing to stretch, test, and revise inherited traditions for a new day. Strong narrative leaders must be steeped in religious tradition, but confident of its elasticity.

These four principles of narrative leadership in ministry and congregational life provide a defining framework for how narrative retrieval, reconstruction, and presentation in ministry unfold. Given these principles about *time, collaboration, genre,* and *canon,* what are the implications for forming narrative leaders in ministry today?

Implications for Educating Narrative Leaders

~

Each of the principles for narrative leadership has implications for how educators and others form narrative leaders today. I had the privilege of serving as part of the research team for the Carnegie Foundation's study of clergy education, published as *Educating Clergy: Teaching Practices and Pastoral Imagination.* In that study, the research team identified four basic pedagogies of contemporary clergy education: *interpretation, formation, contextualization,* and *performance.*[33] Each of these pedagogies has strong narrative components that are illumined and extended by the principles of narrative leadership.

Pedagogies of *interpretation* in seminaries often focus on historical, literary, and sociological methods of critique that value analysis and objectivity over understanding and engagement. Narrative leaders must be guided through all stages of interpretation—a critical distancing from their first naivete of pious assumptions and toward the second naivete of embraced, postcritical understanding. Views of time in textual interpretation must move between the *then* (diachronic) and the *now* (synchronic) so that clergy and laity can cultivate a critical identification with the sacred texts of their tradition. In addition, the horizons of interpretation should vary: from that of personal appropriation, to communal practices and worldviews, to those of the wider values and norms of the religious tradition. In order for narrative leaders to understand sacred texts in relation to self, others, and communities, interpretive pedagogies must cultivate a rich symbolic intelligence about how the text speaks through cultural, historical, and theological imagery. Learning to trust the text in the hands of the community so that they can share in its interpretation is crucial to developing congregation-based practices of collaborative reading and understanding. Finally, learning to identify multiple genres within biblical and talmudic texts—irony, tragedy, comedy, and more—is essential to opening the diversity of witnesses and renditions of the faith. Sometimes, holding open the paradox of differing interpretations of major figures like the patriarchs or prophets, Paul or Jesus—depending on which genre one uses—creates enough space for canonical disruption and recreation to take place.

Pedagogies of *formation*—which focus on awareness of God, lived holiness, and leadership roles—are also transformed by the principles of time, collaboration, genre, and canon in narrative leadership. Clergy and other religious leaders must be formed in varied understandings of time in relation to their pastoral identity. They must form a personal understanding of God's call and direction in their own lives while they identify with a larger sweep of "traditioned time" in the ecclesial or synagogue communities. Clergy and laity must also develop a personal intelligence about sacred texts and traditions so that the texts authentically speak to their own lives and can be shared as resources for the personal formation of others. Formative pedagogies can cultivate a leadership role of guide rather than guardian of the sacred texts and traditions, as leaders learn to usher others into reading, discerning, and practicing their meanings for their own lives. This collaborative work of interpreting and appropriating tradition and practices means that different genres will take hold in different people, and that genres sometimes will clash. Triumphant and heroic views of Jesus's cross, for example, may appeal to certain personalities, while the irony of power in weakness may appeal to others. Finally, formational pedagogies can help leaders realize the elasticity of tradition by identifying the numerous ways they have renegotiated the tradition in their own lives and in the lives of exemplary leaders and saints from history.

Pedagogies of *contextualization* that focus on contextual awareness, encounter, and transformation are also affected by the principles of narrative leadership. Contextual studies of texts, characters, and ministry settings must balance urgent trends of the present with a long view of how the given context is shaped over time. What time framework is chosen to capture the context's characteristics may vary: is it an organic picture of health and decline or a prophetic picture of crisis and opportunity? The more the context's own time is rendered with hope, the more opportunities can arise for collaborative engagement with its future. Narrative leaders must be shaped as resources for and coparticipants in cultural and systemic change, not as experts or fixers of the situation. Perhaps the greatest challenge for contextual pedagogies is to reclaim the congregation as a center of social and religious leadership in its own context, if not a portal for construing a new vision of the neighborhood or community around them. Discerning which genres are at work in how a context is depicted often exposes whose version of the story one is dealing with. Established benefactors of the community may form a story of heroic embattlement, for example, while rising contributors and newcomers may tell a comic tale or ironic story of a struggle for power. Part of the disruptive power of contextual storytelling lies in the ability to expose moral responsibility in times of great change or to open opportunities for new moral and spiritual agency.

Pedagogies of *performance*—which focus on the scripts, community-leader interaction, style, and telos of one's practice—are greatly enhanced by the principles of time, collaboration, genre, and canon in narrative leadership. The way a story is presented can help people recognize the *kairos* time of how an episode or a moment in their lives captures the fullness of God's purpose for them. Inviting others to share in the retrieval, retellings, and new endings of established stories in the tradition or congregation is a powerful act of trust and leadership. Helping pastors claim genres that open the future as one of promise and hope, against final judgment or fatalism, is one task of performative pedagogies. Learning to trust that the religious tradition or congregational history will hold if reworked by the community at large, including newcomers, is one of the goals that performative practices can engender. The more that pastors, priests, and rabbis are coached in taking on the story of Scripture or tradition as their own story and valuing their own retelling and embodying of that story, the more they will begin to trust others around them to do the same. In the end, trusting the congregation to test and weigh various renditions of the religious tradition and its own practices will go a long way toward developing the entrepreneurial practice and creativity necessary for effective narrative leaders.

Never Too Soon to Practice

⁓

While most seminary programs and lay institutes for ministry leadership have to focus on the foundations of necessary knowledge, skills, and norms of ministry in a religious tradition, we at Alban believe the improvisational use and adaptation of one's religious traditions and practices can never begin too soon. While certain academic, spiritual, and pastoral disciplines have to be developed in new seminarians and lay leaders, it is important to begin coaching them early in the range of interpretations, formative patterns, contextual embodiments, and performance styles that the tradition or practice has undergone in its own lifetime. While most seminarians will graduate as beginner or basically competent practitioners, they will have begun the art of improvisation, adaptation, and contextual judgment that identifies the truly competent, if not master, practitioner. Seminary and lay education programs can utilize narrative work and leadership to help develop this improvisational style and adaptive judgment in the established fields and tracks of their existing programs. Advanced programs in DMin and continuing education can focus on these improvisational arts and judgments in ministry, especially through a focus on narrative retrieval, reconstruction, and presentation. The more a growing priest, pastor, rabbi, or lay leader internalizes his or her tradition as one's own theological and spiritual repertoire for ministry, the more they will be poised to deliver effective narrative leadership in their ministry settings.

In this chapter I have shared narrative approaches in psychology, education, and leadership theory that can enhance those already underway in theological education. By combining various narrative theories and practices from these fields, a new framework for ministry can be developed that affirms the power of religious tradition, congregational practice, and deep narrative work in an interactive framework. As ministry practitioners further this art of narrative leadership, the church, synagogue, and academy will learn more about how to form narrative leaders for revitalizing congregational life and practice.

Notes

~

1. Paul Auster, *The Locked Room* (New York: Penguin, 1986).

2. Jean-Francois Lyotard, *The Postmodern Condition: A Report on Knowledge* (Minneapolis: University of Minnesota Press, 1984).

3. Kenneth Gergen, *The Saturated Self: Dilemmas of Contemporary Life* (New York: Basic Books, 1992).

4. Charles Taylor, *Sources of the Self: The Making of Modern Identity* (Cambridge, MA: Harvard University Press, 1989), 289.

5. See Hans Frei, *The Eclipse of Biblical Narrative: A Study of Eighteenth and Nineteenth Century Hermeneutics* (New Haven: Yale University Press, 1980) and *Theology and Narrative: Selected Essays*, ed. George Hunsinger and William C. Placher (New York: Oxford University Press, 1993); Paul Ricoeur, *Hermeneutics and the Human*

Sciences: Essays on Language, Action, and Interpretation, ed. and trans. John B. Thompson (Cambridge: Cambridge University Press, 1981) and *Time and Narrative*, vols. 1–3 (Chicago: University of Chicago Press, 1990); David Tracy, *The Analogical Imagination: Christian Theology and the Culture of Pluralism* (New York: Crossroad, 1981). Others followed one school or another, or tried to combine their aims: George W. Stroup, *The Promise of Narrative Theology: Recovering the Gospel in the Church* (Eugene, OR: Wipf and Stock, 1997); Ronald Thiemann, *Revelation and Theology: The Gospel as Narrated Promise* (Notre Dame, IN: University of Notre Dame Press, 1987); Stanley Hauerwas and L. Gregory Jones, eds., *Why Narrative? Readings in Narrative Theology* (Eugene, OR: Wipf and Stock, 1997); Michael Goldberg, *Theology and Narrative: A Critical Introduction* (Eugene, OR: Wipf and Stock, 2001); Darrell J. Fasching, *Narrative Theology after Auschwitz: From Alienation to Ethics* (Gainesville: University Press of Florida, 2002); Dwight Hopkins and George Cummings, eds., *Cut Loose Your Stammering Tongue: Black Theology in the Slave Narratives* (Louisville, KY: Westminster John Knox, 2003); and Mary Doak, *Reclaiming Narrative for Public Theology* (New York: SUNY, 2004).

6. While these approaches differ, they all share a concern for narrative readings of Scripture: Robert Alter, *The Art of Biblical Narrative* (New York: Basic Books, 1983); Richard Hays, *Echoes of Scripture in the Letters of Paul* (New Haven, CT: Yale University Press, 1989); Brevard Childs, *Introduction to the Old Testament as Scripture* (Minneapolis: Fortress Press, 1989) and *The New Testament as Canon: An Introduction* (Valley Forge, PA: Trinity Press International, 1994); David M. Gunn and Danna Nolan Fewell, *Narrative in the Hebrew Bible*, Oxford Bible Series (New York: Oxford University Press, 1993); Walter Brueggemann, *Theology of the Old Testament: Testimony, Dispute, Advocacy* (Minneapolis: Fortress Press, 1997); John R. Donahue, *The Gospel in Parable: Metaphor, Narrative, and Theology in the Synoptic Gospels* (Minneapolis: Fortress Press, 1990); Frank McConnell, ed., *The Bible and the Narrative Tradition* (New York: Oxford University Press, 1991); James L. Resseguie, *Narrative Criticism of the New Testament: An Introduction* (Grand Rapids: Baker Academic, 2005); and Gail R. O'Day, *The World Disclosed: Preaching the Gospoel of John* (St. Louis, MO: Chalice Press, 2002).

7. Michael White and David Epston, *Narrative Means to Therapeutic Ends* (New York: W. W. Norton, 1990); Andrew D. Lester, *Hope in Pastoral Care and Counseling* (Louisville, KY: Westminster John Knox, 1995); Donald Capps, *Living Stories: Pastoral Counseling in a Congregational Context* (Minneapolis: Augsburg Fortress, 1998); Christie Neuger, *Counseling Women: A Narrative, Pastoral Approach* (Minneapolis: Augsburg Fortress, 2001); and Archie Smith Jr. and Ursula Riedel-Pfaefflin, *Siblings by Choice: Race, Gender, and Violence* (St. Louis: Chalice Press, 2004).

8. Fred Craddock, *Overhearing the Gospel* (Nashville: Abingdon Press, 1979); Eugene L. Lowry, *The Homiletical Plot: The Sermon as Narrative Art Form* (Louisville, KY: Westminster John Knox, 1980); Charles Campbell, *Preaching Jesus: New Directions for Homiletics in Hans Frei's Postliberal Theology* (Grand Rapids: Eerdmans, 1997); David L. Larsen, *Telling the Old, Old Story: The Art of Narrative Preaching* (Grand Rapids: Kregel, 2001); and Joel B. Green and Michael Pasquarello III, eds., *Narrative Reading, Narrative Preaching: Reuniting New Testament Interpretation and Proclamation* (Grand Rapids: Baker Academic, 2003).

9. David N. Power, *Unsearchable Riches: The Symbolic Nature of Liturgy* (Eugene, OR: Wipf and Stock, 2008); Joyce Ann Zimmerman, *Liturgy and Hermeneutics* (Collegeville, MN: Liturgical Press, 1998); and Herbert Anderson and Edward Foley, *Mighty Stories, Dangerous Rituals: Weaving Together the Human and the Divine* (San Francisco: Jossey-Bass, 1998).

10. James F. Hopewell, *Congregation: Stories and Structures* (Philadelphia: Fortress Press, 1987).

11. Nancy Tatom Ammerman, *Congregation and Community* (New Brunswick, NJ: Rutgers University Press, 1987); Ammerman et al, *Studying Congregations* (Nashville: Abingdon Press, 1998). See also the predecessor volume, Jackson W. Carroll et al, *Handbook for Congregational Studies* (Nashville: Abingdon Press, 1986); Penny Becker and Nancy Eiesland, *Contemporary American Religion: An Ethnographic Reader* (Walnut Creek, CA: Alta Mira, 1997); Jackson Carroll et al, *Carriers of Faith: Lessons from Congregational Studies* (Louisville, KY: Westminster John Knox, 1991); Carl Dudley and Nancy Ammerman, *Congregations in Transition: A Guide for Analyzing, Assessing, and Adapting in Changing Communities* (San Fran-

cisco: Jossey-Bass, 2002); and James P. Wind and James W. Lewis, eds., *American Congregations*, 2 vols. (Chicago: University of Chicago Press, 1994).

12. Dorothy Bass, *Practicing Our Faith: A Way of Life for a Searching People* (San Francisco: Jossey-Bass, 1998); Marislav Volf and Dorothy Bass, eds., *Practicing Theology: Beliefs and Practices in Christian Life* (Grand Rapids: Eerdmans, 2002); and Diana Butler Bass and Joseph Stewart-Sicking, *From Nomads to Pilgrims: Stories from Practicing Congregations* (Herndon, VA: Alban Institute, 2005).

13. Michael Polanyi, *The Tacit Dimension* (Gloucester, MA: Peter Smith, 1983).

14. Alasdair MacIntyre, *After Virtue: A Study in Moral Theory* (Notre Dame, IN: University of Notre Dame Press, 1984), 207.

15. Diana Butler Bass, *Christianity for the Rest of Us: How the Neighborhood Church Is Transforming Faith* (San Francisco: HarperSanFrancisco, 2006), 11.

16. Diana Butler Bass, *The Practicing Congregation: Imagining a New Old Church* (Herndon, VA: Alban Institute, 2004), 95.

17. Ibid., 97.

18. Ibid., 98.

19. Dan P. McAdams, *The Redemptive Self: Stories Americans Live By* (New York: Oxford University Press, 2006), 42.

20. Erik Erikson, *Identity and the Life Cycle* (New York: Norton, 1959).

21. McAdams, *Redemptive Self*, 49.

22. Ibid., 61–70.

23. Jerome Bruner, *The Culture of Education* (Cambridge, MA: Harvard University Press, 1996) and *Making Stories: Law, Literature, Life* (Cambridge, MA: Harvard University Press, 2003).

24. Bruner, *Culture of Education*, 40.

25. Ibid., 133. See also Ricoeur, *Time and Narrative*, vol. 1 (Chicago: University of Chicago Press, 1984).

26. Bruner, *Culture of Education*, 136.

27. Bruner accepts the four basic genres identified by Northrop Frye in *Anatomy of Criticism: Four Essays* (Princeton, NJ: Princeton University Press, 1957). See also Frye's relation of classic genres to the Bible in *The Great Code: The Bible and Literature* (New York: Harcourt Brace, 1983), 134.

28. Hopewell, *Congregation*.

29. Bruner, *Culture of Education*, 139.

30. Ibid., 142.

31. Howard Gardner, *Leading Minds: The Anatomy of Leadership* (New York: HarperCollins, 1996) and *Changing Minds: The Art And Science of Changing Our Own and Other People's Minds* (Boston: Harvard Business School Press, 2006).

32. The African threefold method is based upon reading, reacting, and responding with key words and insights about God's call from each participant.

33. Charles Foster, Lisa Dahill, Lawrence Golemon, and Barbara Wang Tolentino, *Educating Clergy: Teaching Practices and Pastoral Imagination* (San Francisco: Jossey-Bass, 2006), 67–186.

CHAPTER 2

The Official
and Unofficial Story

A NARRATIVE OF IDENTITY
AND FAITHFULNESS IN THE BIBLE

⁓

JUDY FENTRESS-WILLIAMS

When asked to write an autobiographical sketch—a brief narrative that includes some of the salient points from my curriculum vitae—I have always felt challenged. Designed for the listener rather than the reader, the sketch should tell the audience not only who you are but also why people might want to listen to you or read your work. The narrative includes your educational accomplishments, your current vocation, your published works, organizations you belong to, and some mention of your interests and family life. It is an "official," albeit selective, rendering of your existence. If someone wanted to know who you were, this sketch should provide some information about you that would make you at least recognizable, if not familiar.

Unfortunately, these official renderings do not reveal all of a person's identity. Much of who we are comes from our "unofficial" stories, the ones our siblings might tell about us. These unofficial stories do not readily fit the image the official story creates. In fact, these stories tend to circulate in two different spheres so that if we are not careful, our public and private identities come to resemble each other less and less. The two traditions lay claim to parts of the narrative identity, and if they remain separate, each narrative lacks pertinent information and has gaps. An example would be the "self-made" man whose spouse toiled in obscurity so that he could be successful. Often the unofficial narrative reveals motivations and circumstances behind our accomplishments that we unintentionally forgot or wish could be forgotten.

Forgetfulness is a part of the human condition. Although we sometimes unintentionally forget, sometimes we choose to forget because we do not want to remember. We intentionally leave out aspects of the story because they are too painful to recall. Depending on our audience, we frame our story in a particular way, choosing the lens through which to interpret events. This selective storytelling is reflected in national identity. The United States, for example, tends to tell its story from the perspective of victor or winner so that its failures and disappointments are minimized, excluded, or recast as part of a larger victory. The histories that Americans wrote immediately after the Vietnam War were reluctant to say that the United States was not victorious, and this was due, in part, to the country's lack of both vocabulary and mindset to do so.

Scripture is a corrective to selective storytelling because it includes both the official and unofficial voices. Traditions sit alongside the countertraditions, and these narratives form a dialogue around, among other things, Israel's identity. In fact, Deuteronomy commands the people to maintain an identity that includes their experience in the wilderness. This command then directs Israel and her children to remember their story as one that includes homelessness, wandering, and uncertainty.

Narrative and Identity in Deuteronomy

The book of Deuteronomy is a long narrative sermon perched on the edge of promise. As the last book of the Torah, it provides a conclusion to this first division of the Bible while setting the stage for the second division, the Prophets. In the canon, it functions as a "swing book," permanently occupying liminal space. Geographically, Deuteronomy takes place on the border between the wilderness and the land of promise. With the exception of the account of Moses's death, Deuteronomy adds little to the overall narrative of the Torah. This book is a pause, a moment between the action of wandering in the wilderness and the action of entering Canaan. Moses tells Israel her story at this particular moment because it is central to her formation and identity as a people.

The command to remember is in tension with the human tendency to forget. When Israel enters the land of promise, she will go from being a sojourner (*ger*) to a nation, a people of the land. In anticipation of this transition, Moses recounts the history of Israel in the wilderness. The sermonic history of Deuteronomy is filled with the commands to "Hear," "Take care," "Don't forget," and "Remember," because memory is key to identity. The repetition of these commands assumes forgetfulness, and this is a realistic assumption. While in the wilderness, Israel's memory was faulty. The people's story was filled with incidents of forgetting the commands or forgetting to keep them.

A closer examination of Moses's command to remember reveals a call to a specific memory. Moses wants Israel to take the memory of the wilderness into the land of promise. This is a rather peculiar request. One would imagine that after forty years of struggle in the wilderness, the people would like nothing more than to forget this difficult past. Yet, Moses's sermon makes numerous references to the people's experience in the wilderness as they prepare to leave it (Deut. 6:10–12; 8:1–6; 9:6–29). The lessons of the desert are a part of the story that must not be lost in the potential prosperity of the promised land.

Ironically, Deuteronomy, the very book in which these instructions are recorded, is likely the lost and forgotten scroll referred to in 2 Kings 22:8–10. When Josiah read the book that was found in the Temple, he wept upon realizing what had been forgotten. Without the book the people had forgotten rules that were central to their identity as God's people. The recovery of the book led to a massive reform (2 Kings 23:1–25).

As the story of Josiah and the lost book illustrates, memory is key to identity. The ability to remember or recover what has been forgotten or lost is key to survival. This pattern of remembering and forgetting also describes the act of interpretation. Interpretation is "an activity of repressing and reconstructing, of forgetting and remembering and that activity, by its very nature resists completion."[1] This means that a community's survival is tied to its memory—that is, its retrieval and interpretation of past events.

Remembering the wilderness protects against a history and identity based only on victories and moments of strength. If the wilderness experience is used to inform Israel's identity, Israel becomes, among other things, vulnerable, disobedient, willful, and afraid. In the wilderness she is utterly dependent upon God. In the wilderness Israel experienced God's provision, protection, and guidance. Moses's message in Deuteronomy is clear—forgetting the wilderness would mean forgetting the faithfulness of God.

The command to remember in Deuteronomy is tied to the command to teach, tell, and repeat Israel's story. This telling and retelling is not intended to happen in a vacuum, rather Israel is commanded to tell the story to her children so that they can tell the story. As the children hear and then tell the story, they make it their own. In Deuteronomy, the sharing of the story allows each member of the community to make this history and the covenant that supports it his or her own. By repeating the shared story, each person finds his or her place in the history and in the community. Israel's ability to keep this commandment—the remembering, retelling, and repetition of the exodus sojourn in the wilderness and the entry to the promised land—transformed the historical event. The events of redemption and sojourn towards home become literary motif. These are the dominant rubrics used by Israel to tell a story that is not limited to past events but is ongoing.

Narrative and Identity in Ruth

With the Deuteronomistic command to remember as a background, I will examine Israel's story of Ruth. Ruth is one of the best known and often repeated stories of the Hebrew Bible. This short book contains the elements of loss and recovery—famine and harvest, barrenness and fruitfulness, life and death—requiring the characters in the narrative to interpret their context in order to establish or maintain an identity. Ruth is an official and unofficial story about identity. It is official in that it concludes with a brief genealogy that leads to King David. It is unofficial because the main characters are women (Naomi and Ruth), they are widows, and Ruth is a Moabite. Thus Ruth provides a model for remembering a story so that one's identity is informed by weakness and strength, victory and failure. For the women in this story, interpretation is an act of survival. Against a changing backdrop, they engage in a dialogue of interpretation that allows them to define and redefine their identity, and in so doing come to understand the core values that constitute identity.

The story of Ruth uses two motifs to explore identity: the journey toward home and redemption. Israel's identity is based on the call and promise that included a homeland. Like the Israelites on the verge of entering Canaan, the shifts recounted in the Ruth narrative require the characters to interpret and reinterpret their context in order to establish and maintain an identity. In this story, the reader is invited to explore the issues of identity when the constructs that traditionally inform identity are missing.

The book of Ruth appears in the third division of the Hebrew Bible, *Ketuvim*. The book is associated with the celebration of *Shevu'ot*, the feast of weeks.[2] The Septuagint placed Ruth in the second division of the Bible, *nevi'im*, or prophets, immediately after the book of Judges because the book begins with the phrase, "In the days that the judges ruled . . ." However, the language in Ruth suggests a later date than Judges. Another possibility is that Ruth was written as a response to the strident prohibition against intermarriage as recorded in Ezra and Nehemiah. Thus, Ruth occupies different places in the canon and is associated with celebration or festival, judges and the period of time preceding the monarchy, and the postexilic period of Ezra and Nehemiah. By its various placements, Ruth has a number of external dialogue partners.

Ruth is full of dialogue. The majority of the book of Ruth (fifty-five of the eighty-five verses) is comprised of direct speech. This dialogue in Ruth does more than advance the plot of the narrative. The series of exchanges between Naomi, Ruth, Orpah, Boaz, and the people of Bethlehem are all connected by the theme of identity. For the women in this story, establishing identity is an act of survival. It is a performance, a demonstration of the way interpretation is life giving.

Dialogue between characters is indicative of the very nature of biblical narrative. Dialogue reminds readers and listeners that the Bible itself is utterly dialogic. The various voices in the text are involved in an ongoing conversation. Every word carries a multitude of possible meanings, and perception or understanding is affected by the presence of another. Earlier traditions are in dialogue with later traditions to speak to a truth that is larger than any single tradition. In the case of the book of Ruth, the various placements of the book in the canon form dialogues. In a dialogue, the presence of another speaker brings with it a new field of vision or perspective:

Regardless of the position and the proximity to me of this other human being whom I am contemplating I shall always see and know something that he, from his place outside and over against me, cannot see himself: parts of his body that are inaccessible to his own gaze (his head, his face and its expression) the world behind his back . . . are accessible to me but not to him. As we gaze at each other, two different worlds are reflected in the pupils of our eyes . . . to annihilate the difference completely, it would be necessary to merge into one, to become one and the same person.[3]

In the book of Ruth, the series of dialogues involving Ruth, Naomi, and Boaz demonstrate that their identities, their status or place in society, are affected by the encounter or dialogue with the other characters. Because dialogue expands the horizon of the individual, the dialogue forms bridges across the constructs that usually determine identity. The dialogues allow us to chart the shift in Ruth's identity from outsider to a respected and honored member of the family.

The first dialogic exchange is the best known of the dialogues in the book of Ruth. Verses 1 through 6 of chapter 1 provide the setting. Elimelech and his family, Naomi, Mahlon, and Chilion, leave Bethlehem because of a famine and sojourn to Moab. Elimelech dies in the land of Moab, and Naomi is left with her sons, who marry Moabite women, Orpah and Ruth. After a period of time (ten years), the sons Mahlon and Chilion die. Naomi and her daughters-in-law are left behind. Around this time, Naomi receives word that the famine in Bethlehem is over and she starts off for Bethlehem with her daughters-in-law. All of this information comes to the reader through the narrator. In these few verses, the narrator not only gives a summary of the action in the plot but also exposes the constructs under which identity is formed in these societies. In this society women have restricted movement. They are daughters, wives, mothers, mothers-in-law, daughters-in-law, and widows. In other words, they are bound to and dependent upon the men in their families. The narrative also reveals that there are Israelites and there are others, in this case, Moabites.

In verse 7, Naomi and her daughters-in-law were "on their way to go back to the land of Judah." It is after she embarks on the return that Naomi orders her daughters to do the same, to *go back* home, to their "mother's house." Both daughters-in-law resist and assert that they will *go back* with Naomi, to her people. Here Naomi reasons with them, speaking the refrain, "*Turn back*," reminding them that she has no other sons and the prospects of them procuring husbands is slim. For them to return with her is unreasonable because she has nothing to offer them. Naomi's argument is based on the existing constructs that shape identity in this culture. All three of them are widows, which makes them vulnerable. That her daughters-in-law are foreigners exacerbates the situation.

This dialogue is marked by repetition of the verb *sub*, which is translated as *go back, turn back,* and *return.* This word is replete with meaning. For the audience that heard this story in or after the exile, the word *sub* characterized the desire to return home from the place of exile.

The location of this dialogue is significant. Naomi is on her way back home with her daughters-in-law. After the journey is begun, Naomi pauses, almost as an afterthought. It is as if they have gone as far as they can together—in a literary sense, they have come to the end of what the societal constructs can allow for them. Moabite widows do not belong in Bethlehem; and as the women approached Bethlehem, it may have become evident to Naomi that in this other location her daughters-in-law would take on an identity that would be a hindrance. They are at a crossroads.

Orpah sees the logic of Naomi's argument and, after weeping, kisses her mother-in-law. Ruth, however, does not let go, and so Naomi attempts to convince her again, this time pointing out that Orpah has gone back and that she should as well. Verse 16 records Ruth's response to Naomi's plea:

Do not press me to leave you
　　or to *turn back* from following you!
Where you go, I will go;
　　Where you lodge, I will lodge;
your people shall be my people,
　　and your God my God.
Where you die, I will die—
　　there will I be buried.
May the LORD do thus and so to me,
　　and more as well,
if even death parts me from you!

Ruth's response to Naomi consists of five sets of doublets or parallel lines that end in a vow. The doublets have these word pairs: *leave/turn back, go/lodge, people/God, die/buried*. The first doublet is a negative command; the following three are a declaration. These three doublets in the middle intentionally place Naomi (*you*) first. The language reflects the force of the statement. Naomi will be followed by Ruth. Ruth is bound to Naomi. The dialogue ends with Ruth's words. The narrator tells us Naomi said nothing in response to Ruth's words because "she saw that she was determined to go with her" (1:18).

Ruth's words supply a response to Naomi, albeit an unreasonable one. Ruth clings to Naomi out of loyalty. She makes the decision that her future and fate will be tied to Naomi, Naomi's people, and Naomi's God. In this exchange, Ruth's response tells us that identity is shaped by more than one's location and nationality but by one's choices. Ruth chooses an identity that is based on faithfulness, *hesed*.

Prior to this moment, the women were brought together by circumstances of famine and marriage. Now Ruth makes an intentional commitment, evoking the language of covenant. They have reached the limits of where they can go with their current identities, and Ruth attaches her identity to Naomi. She understands that if they are to continue on together, their

current identities must be surrendered or altered. The language
of covenant is intentional. The covenant is the bond that holds
together another unlikely pair, namely God and God's people.
It is God's persistence and faithfulness that have allowed Israel
to continue.

The encounter between Ruth and Naomi evokes the setting
for the book of Deuteronomy. Naomi is poised to return home
to the land of promise in much the same way the children of
Israel were prepared to enter this land once known as Canaan.
Moses asks the people to take the memory of the wilderness
with them and Ruth asks Naomi to take her, a vivid reminder
to Naomi of her loss, her childlessness, and her recent past as
a sojourner. If Naomi allows Ruth to accompany her, she will
be fundamentally altered. Similarly, Ruth's words demonstrate
her understanding that her choice to stay with Naomi will require a shift in her identity.

In choosing to stay with Naomi, Ruth is doing more than
choosing a new identity. Her words demonstrate a new construct for her identity. From now own, faithfulness, not ethnic
background or husband, will be the construct that will inform
identity. Ruth's faithfulness makes her vulnerable, and it is
countercultural, but it is also the basis upon which the characters' lives are transformed.

With dialogue, new constructs can come into being, with
endless possibilities. The work of dialogue affords us the opportunity to envision new worlds through those with whom
we engage in dialogue, but this exchange demands something
of us. Dialogue requires that we surrender the right to a single
perspective. We offer our vision as we receive that of our neighbor. This sharing of perspective makes possible the creation of
new communities that are not limited by societal constructs.

In the narrative action that follows Ruth's vow, faithfulness becomes the primary factor that determines her identity.
Ruth's faithfulness gets the attention of the redeemer Boaz, and
she is rewarded with a family (husband and son) that provides
stability for her and Naomi. It should be noted that Ruth's

faithfulness is directed toward a purpose that is larger than her own circumstances. Ruth is praised as being worth more to Naomi "than seven sons" (4:15). The child she bears is placed on Naomi's breast and is her heir. The narrative then shifts to give the genealogy that leads to David, son of Jesse. Ruth's faithfulness is the deciding factor in a story of national importance. That means, ultimately, the book of Ruth is not about Ruth, but the work of God.

The Politics of Personhood

In this first chapter of Ruth, we observe two journeys. The first is the one undertaken by Elimelech and his family as they leave their home in search of food. This first journey involves leaving the place to which their identity is rooted. While they are sojourners in Moab, Naomi's sons marry Moabite women. Intermarriage is counter to their identity as Israelites. Finally, Naomi's husband and sons die, and she and these Moabite daughters-in-law lose a primary indicator of identity, the men who inherit on their behalf and provide for them. This first journey is one in which identity based on homeland, marriage within one's people (for the sons), and marriage (for the women) is lost.

Naomi embarks on a second journey when there is food in her homeland, but she returns barren, stripped of the things around which her identity was built. When she attempts to send her daughters-in-law back, Ruth clings to her and, in so doing, forms a new basis for identity. Chapter 1:14 states, "but Ruth clung to her." The word here for clung, *dbq*, is used to describe the union of a husband and wife. Here the very vocabulary demands a new understanding of words associated with traditional constructs. In other words, the narrator uses a word traditionally associated with a woman and a man in marriage to describe Ruth's bond with Naomi. Ruth will remain with

Naomi because of faithfulness, and this act will set into motion a course of events that will result in their redemption.

This shift is accomplished through dialogue. Ruth responds to Naomi's command to leave with a new construct of faithfulness that exceeds cultural constraints. The dialogue in this chapter and throughout the narrative explores the existing constructs of identity over and against the faithfulness of Ruth. Ruth's faithfulness represents God's faithfulness to Israel in the wilderness. God's faithfulness, like that of Ruth, is not bound by the cultural constructs of location, nationality, or gender. It is the core, ongoing value of Israel's identity.

Ruth's decision to stay with Naomi demands an adjustment of identity on the part of Naomi, as does the return home. Upon the women's return to Bethlehem, the townspeople take notice of Naomi and Ruth. The women said, "Is this Naomi?" to which she responded:

> Call me no longer Naomi,
>   call me Mara,
> for the Almighty has dealt bitterly with me.
> I went away full,
>   but the LORD has brought me back empty;
> why call me Naomi
>   when the LORD has dealt harshly with me,
> and the Almighty has brought calamity upon me? (1:20–21)

In this dialogue, the women of Bethlehem raise a question about Naomi's identity. We know that while she was away from home, Naomi lost that part of her identity tied to her husband and her sons. What is not clear in the text is the basis for the women of Bethlehem's lack of recognition. Is it her widow's attire? Does she bear the effects of the famine? Is it simply the passage of time or is it the presence of the strange young widow who accompanies her? What is clear is that Naomi chooses a name that reflects her state of bitterness, *Mara*. This name forms a dialogue with Exodus 15:22–27, the account of the bitter waters the Israelites encounter after leaving Egypt. In the exodus narrative, the people are without water. After following Moses in the wilderness, they come to bitter water, which is appropriately called *Marah* (15:23). What is of interest in this narrative is that the people are led by God to the bitter waters of Marah and, after making the water drinkable, God sets the rules for their relationship. In Exodus 15:26, God says, "If you will listen carefully to the voice of the LORD your God, and do what is right in his sight, and give heed to his commandments and keep all his statutes, I will not bring upon you any of the diseases that I brought upon the Egyptians; for I am the LORD who heals you." In Exodus, God sets the terms for relating to Israel against the backdrop of blessing versus plague, water versus wilderness. It is a liminal moment. Similarly, the reference to Mara in Ruth acknowledges the fact that although Naomi has returned home, her identity is not certain and her future is not secure. When her identity is questioned by those who knew her years ago, she embraces the identity of loss. The identity of loss is only one part of Naomi's story. What is not reflected in her response (because she does not know this) is the possibility that exists in and through the faithfulness of the Moabite widow by her side.

The dialogue around identity (in changing situations) is raised in the next chapter where a series of exchanges occur. The first and last exchanges in the chapter are between Ruth and Naomi (2:2; 2:19–22). In the first, Ruth informs Naomi that she intends to glean a nearby field and Naomi affirms her wish. In the concluding dialogue in this chapter, Ruth reports to Naomi about her successful endeavor and her fortuitous encounter with Boaz, who, as luck would have it (v. 3), is a relative. These exchanges form an envelope around the two encounters between Ruth and Boaz. In verse 5, Boaz notices Ruth among the gleaners and asks, "To whom does this young woman belong?" The question is one of identity. Ruth's identity is tied to the person to whom she belongs. The response is, "She is the Moabite who came back with Naomi from the land of Moab" (v. 6). Ruth belongs to the land of Moab and Naomi. Armed with this information, Boaz speaks to Ruth directly, telling her where to glean and allowing her some privileges afforded his workers. Boaz's instructions create another shift in her identity. She is a gleaner who is to be treated like one of Boaz's workers. In response to his generosity, Ruth asks, "Why have I found favor in your sight, that you should take notice of me, when I am a foreigner?" (v. 10).

Boaz's response provides us with direction: "All that you have done for your mother-in-law since the death of your husband has been fully told me, and how you left your father and mother and your native land and came to a people that you did not know before. May the LORD reward you for your deeds, and may you have a full reward from the LORD, the God of Israel, under whose wings you have come for refuge! (vv. 11–12).

Boaz's treatment of Ruth does not make sense based on her national identity. For Boaz, the key to determining her identity at this point is Ruth's *hesed*, or faithfulness to her mother-in-law. Faithfulness, the basis upon which Ruth is tied to Naomi in chapter 1, is the same basis upon which Boaz extends kindness to the Moabite widow in chapter 2. Boaz calls her "daughter" (2:8), which conveys kindness and may also speak to the difference in their ages.

Chapter 3 has three exchanges that continue the dialogue around identity. The first and the third are between Ruth and Naomi and the second is between Ruth and Boaz. As was the case in the preceding chapter, the first and third dialogues form bookends around the central exchange, where the course of Ruth's future status and identity will be determined. Here the nature of the dialogue takes a decisive turn. If in the first two chapters, identity is questioned or named, in the final two chapters, dialogue is used to ensure that this new identity or status is realized.

First Naomi instructs Ruth out of the need to secure their future. Naomi speaks in verses 1–4, giving Ruth a series of instructions on what she is to do on the threshing floor. Ruth simply responds, "All that you tell me I will do" (v. 5). Unlike the first exchange in chapter 1 (vv. 15–18) where Naomi tells Ruth to return or go back, Ruth does not resist Naomi's instruction. Once the covenant has been made, the two work as a team, as evidenced in chapter 2. When Naomi shares her plan for their survival, Ruth complies and is willing to follow Naomi's plan as well as Boaz's commands. As Ruth follows Naomi and Boaz's commands, a different kind of family is created. Both Naomi and Boaz refer to Ruth as "daughter," and both of them, up until this point in the narrative, exercise a parental role. Naomi and Boaz are related, but not by marriage. The only way Ruth, the daughter, will be related to either of them is by marriage, which is a covenant. In following Naomi's and Boaz's direction, she becomes the wife of Boaz and the mother of Obed (in chapter 4), who then is associated with Naomi. The identification of the child with Naomi may be an attempt to secure the child's Judaic lineage.[4] The child's name, Obed, means "he who serves." This child of Ruth, Boaz, and Naomi serves a number of purposes. The child born to Ruth and identified with Naomi takes away the stigma of loss to the one who called herself Mara. Moreover, the child's name also reflects his mother's role in the movement of this narrative. Ruth's faithful service restores the family line.

Who Are You?

At each turn in the narrative of Ruth, the shifts in identity are conveyed by using more than one voice. The reader may expect to have an omniscient narrator, but one voice is not adequate to the task. In this narrative, the dialogue takes the lead, and the dialogue is by nature unpredictable. By using a chorus instead of one official voice, the reader is given fuller understanding of the story and is able to explore the complexity of identity. When we tell our story using more than one voice, we do a better job of remembering. Beyond the official or dominant story are the perspectives of the community that come from the margins. The stories of these members are often the stories of the wilderness: those of homelessness and disenfranchisement. The command in Deuteronomy to remember the story of the wilderness is honored in the Ruth narrative because the Moabite is allowed to speak. When the Moabite speaks, the ensuing dialogue allows her to move from "other" to daughter to wife, mother, and honored ancestor.

In this essay, I have formed an intentional dialogue between Deuteronomy and Ruth. Starting with Deuteronomy's unique command to remember as central to identity, I have then examined the dialogue in Ruth to glean directives for creating our own narratives in our communities of faith. The book of Ruth presents us with a narrative that contains both official and unofficial elements. These elements are held together with dialogue. Dialogue allows for a vision of identity that exceeds the traditional cultural constructs of identity. For contemporary communities of faith, the following observations can be made:

- *Deuteronomy reminds us that our shared story of identity should contain official and unofficial elements.* Deuteronomy's command goes against our tendency to present our stories through a rose-colored lens. The unofficial parts of our story are often the places where the work of redemption takes place. God works through and in spite of our shortcomings and our failures. When we eliminate the unofficial elements of our story, we run the risk of establishing a false identity—one that is not based on the faithfulness of God. In a congregation, this is accomplished by giving everyone an opportunity to contribute to the narrative of identity.

‹ *Ruth shows us that covenant is a commitment to relationship and this commitment embodies God's faithfulness.* In chapter 1 of Ruth, Ruth forms a covenant with Naomi. The covenant comes out of a dialogue and reframes the construct of identity so that the relationship between Naomi and Ruth holds more sway than the other markers of identity. In other words, the things that would have made Ruth an outsider are overcome by her faithfulness, her *hesed* to her mother-in-law.

‹ *A commitment to dialogue will require openness to the other and a willingness to see God in new ways.* Faithfulness to dialogue, the commitment to an authentic engagement, demands a level of vulnerability. We reveal ourselves to the other and they to us. In that exchange, we discover new opportunities to experience God's faithfulness.

Notes

1. Regina Schwartz, "Joseph's Bones and the Resurrection of the Text: Remembering in the Bible" in *The Book and the Text: The Bible and Literary Theory*, ed. Regina Schwartz, (Oxford, UK: Blackwell, 1990), 41.

2. The book of Ruth, along with Song of Songs, Lamentations, Ecclesiastes (Qohelet), and Esther, is one of the five "megillot" or scrolls associated with a festival or observation. Shevu'ot is a festival associated with the harvest, and much of the action in the book takes place at the time of harvest.

3. Michael Holquist and Vadim Liapunov, eds., *Art and Answerability: Early Philosophical Essays by M. M. Bakhtin* (Austin: University of Texas Press, 1990), 22–23.

4. Kirsten Nielsen, *Ruth*, trans. Edward Broadbridge, Old Testament Library (Louisville, KY: Westminster John Knox, 1997), 94.

CHAPTER 3

Preaching the Christian Story among Other Faith Stories

A CASE STUDY OF A COURSE

~

SUSAN K. HEDAHL

Ideas come and go, but the stories remain.

—NASSIM NICHOLAS TALEB, *THE BLACK SWAN*

The role of narrative in preaching has a rich and complicated history. This history does not remain simply theoretical and scholarly but is embodied daily in the words of those who exercise the role of public preacher in Christian communities everywhere. In this essay I am defining *narrative* in homiletical terms to mean presenting biblical materials to listeners, through the act of preaching, as a means of shaping individual and corporate faith and of encouraging enactments of mission within and beyond the congregation.

The field of homiletics, as taught in seminaries everywhere, presents the most substantial reminder of the conjunction of gospel and its public presentation in congregations. In many ways, the role of homiletics in seminary curriculum has a taken-for-granted sense: *of course*, these biblical narratives will be taught and learned for retelling in congregational settings.

This general ease of interpretation regarding homiletics, however, masks the increasingly pluralistic, confused, and often
fragmented sense of how gospel should bear meaning in a sermon today. Like turning a kaleidoscope, twenty-first-century
preaching repeatedly takes on a variety of changes and nuances. This means more questions are now on the table about
the role sermonic narrative should play: How does the sermon
and its choice of narratives form congregational life? What are
the relationships among sermonic, biblical, and contemporary
narratives? Who are the presumed listeners to sermons today
and how do they function—even if silently—to shape the narrative of the sermon? What do the narratives of today's public
preaching have to do with the worlds outside the sanctuary
from which the listeners come and to which they will return?

In speaking publicly today as people of the Christian faith,
it is obvious to even the least concerned that preaching the gospel is set within much larger global and international contexts
and concerns. By way of example, it would be a fair assess-
ment of the current religious environment to understand that
preaching the gospel has taken on more the ballast of questions
than answers since the events of what is globally termed 9/11.

We often feel an undefined but acute sense that sermon
listeners and interpretive approaches and claims have shifted
in ways we preachers can only vaguely discern. Christians and
non-Christians alike are questioning the narrative intentionality and intelligibility of how we proclaim our faith in the pulpit.
What, indeed, *is* motivating us? Preachers have a different self-
consciousness about preaching the Gospel narratives, which
was not present a decade ago and has certainly departed radically from the confidence of past decades and centuries.

As a homiletics teacher, I contend that two related questions challenge contemporary Christian homiletics: First, in
which contexts are we Christian preachers now preaching the
Gospel narratives? Second, how do we assess and respond to

the meaning and changes these contexts bring to bear on our preaching? These questions are not merely a replay of the old quip about preaching with the Bible in one hand and the local newspaper in the other, because today the issues are more complicated than ever.

A Course Case Study

To probe these questions, I offered a new course—experimental in nature—for seminary students and pastors in January 2007 at Lutheran Theological Seminary at Gettysburg, Pennsylvania. The major highlights, features, and responses to the course are presented in this section. The next section, "Engaging Sermonic Stories: Rhetorical Revelations," will scrutinize more closely some of the primary issues the course raised in the process of study and class interactions. That section and the one that follows, "Envisioning the Narrative Future: Educational Strategies for Interreligious Comparative Homiletics," will offer significant details about the course with the hope that it can be replicated in various ways in other venues.

The course was entitled "Preaching in the Abrahamic Faith Family: Jewish, Christian, Islamic Proclamation." My reasons for offering the course were multiple. My field of homiletics is based on teaching, researching, and understanding the public faith-narrative genre called sermon, something all three members of the Abrahamic faith family hold in common. My own background in homiletics included education in both Islamic and Jewish proclamation. I had lived in an East African country among Muslims. I had studied several homiletical and scriptural languages, including my ongoing study of Arabic. Our seminary has access to churches, synagogues, and mosques in which students have opportunity to hear the narratives of faith proclaimed. The components of the course, both practical and theoretical, were at hand, driven by my own homiletical curiosity as to how Christian sermonic narratives of the Gospels are now being affected and fashioned through shifts in today's global contexts.

What I was not expecting in my preliminary preparation was finding the complete absence of any such homiletics course in any seminary in the United States. Some comparative religion courses in various seminaries offered work in the Abrahamic faith family, but nothing existed in addressing the scripturally based narratives of faith expressed in preaching. What did any of us—instructor and students—know about how or why our Jewish and Muslim neighbors preached their sermons? As eager as my students, I began the course probing possible answers to this question. This course was indeed a first in what I term interreligious comparative homiletics.

Particularly gratifying was the outpouring of assistance in resources from both Jewish and Islamic sources as I prepared course materials. I began the class with more than sufficient materials from strangers whose letters, phone calls, or e-mails offered me substantial assistance in explaining their own faith's version of homiletics and preaching.

Class participants were a mix of students; approximately half were seminary seniors and the others ordained and involved in ministries ranging from the parish to campus pastoring. The class also contained a mix of Protestant religious traditions. This mix enriched the interactions, because each participant signified different ministry audiences and communities that focused the person's questions and concerns. Of all the homiletics courses I have taught in the last fifteen years, this one provoked the most interaction and comment on the part of students. With a sense of regret, we concluded the class and, with a sense of intrigue, we left bearing many key questions about what had transpired in our comparative homiletics work. What had started as a course in comparative homiletics evolved—is still evolving—into larger issues about the contexts in which Christian preaching speaks today and what the nature of the preachers' intentions might be as we speak our faith narratives from the pulpit.

A ROSE Statement

As with almost all courses at our seminary, the course syllabus was arranged according to the acronym ROSE, which entails a description of rationale, objectives, strategies, and evaluation. I will examine each of the elements in turn.

The *rationale* of the course states: "Preaching is one form of sacred discourse. It is a predominant practice in all three of the Abrahamic faiths. This course will explore the history, characteristics, rhetorical strategies, structures and function of preaching in Jewish, Christian, and Muslim settings, with emphasis on preaching in these communities in contemporary America."

Essential to the course's direction was what the rationale notes—course participants would be looking at a "practice." This meant reading and analyzing contemporary sermons from all three faith traditions. Collecting such sermons took us all on a dizzying journey into personal contacts in different seminaries, library archives, sermon manuscript gifts from different preachers, and the Internet. This was buttressed by the occasional opportunity to speak in person or by e-mail to a preacher and ask, "What does this sermon mean for you and your faith community?" "Why did you write your sermon in this way?" "What do your listeners expect you to preach about?" "What roles does your faith's sacred scripture play in narrating the faith from the pulpit?"

The weeklong intensive course was charted according to the course *objectives*:

At the conclusion of this weeklong intensive course, participants will have engaged:

+ The major characteristics, meanings and functions of preaching in each Abrahamic faith tradition;
+ The role of sacred scripture in the preaching of each tradition;
+ How forms of lectionary cycles shape each tradition's preaching;
+ Rhetorical analysis as a tool for evaluating the written and audio sermons used in the course and final paper;
+ How the preaching traditions compare with one another in their roles in the faith life of each community;
+ An experientially based opportunity to hear worship and preaching in the Islamic tradition;[1]
+ The vast quantity of primary and secondary resources related to preaching in the Abrahamic faith family.

At the conclusion of the course, two major responses to these objectives were that this course should (1) be required for all seminary students prior to graduation and in all degree programs and (2) the course should be a semester in length. One of the patterns class participants fell into, almost accidentally, in our hours together, was keeping our Bibles and Qur'ans in front of us, frequently using both texts to compare the passages noted in sermons and in other readings and to examine primary figures all three scriptures mention, such as Abraham, Moses, and Joseph.

The course's *strategies* included the usual requirements for attendance, verbal and written participation, and a paper. They also included this note: "Maintain a respectful attitude of enquiry. While comparison of personal religious practices and beliefs is definitely encouraged throughout this course, materials foreign to any participant's ways of thinking should not be subject to inappropriate critical attitudes of evangelism or proselytizing responses."

This strategy did not obviate the realities of evangelism and calls to the gospel to which the Christian preacher must respond, but rather it was designed to encourage an open academic attitude in studying other faith perspectives without becoming sidetracked by nonclassroom concerns. Such an approach, however, did not relieve students from considering evangelism questions, which are definitely part of ministerial work and preaching.

The academic fruit of the course was realized in a final paper. Students were asked to compare sermons from each tradition, using rhetorical tools that addressed the words (preacher's and sacred scriptures'), the audience, and the role of the preacher. Some chose sermons that focused on one figure, such as Abraham, while others chose topical sermons addressing such issues as justice, the practices of faithful living, or specific festivals and rituals.

In addition to the multiple sermon sources and materials that students accumulated, everyone in the course was asked to read the following core texts in addition to the Hebrew and Christian scriptures: *Abraham: A Journey to the Heart of Three Faiths* by Bruce Feiler; *The Children of Abraham: Judaism, Christianity, Islam* by F. E. Peters; and *The Meaning of the Holy Qur'an* by Abdullah Yusuf Ali.[2]

This required reading focused on establishing the common themes, stories, and theologies that have created the Abrahamic faith family, called such because they all claim a common religious ancestor in the figure of Abraham. He is represented in some fashion or another in Hebrew, Christian, and Muslim sacred scriptures. Since shared narratives to some extent lead to shared homiletical narratives, focusing the initial readings on this fact was important.

The fashion in which the Abrahamic narrative is told, however, varies with each tradition. Comparing Christian versions of the Abraham story to those of both Jews and Muslims was confusing and exhilarating. The comparative strategies prompted many questions: Is there a core version of the story of Abraham, and which of these faith versions tells it most definitively, if any of them do? Who comes into view in any version of the Abraham story that was in the background or absent in the other versions? Perhaps most happily troubling was the fact that the figure of Abraham, foundational to all three faiths, continues to be reshaped by them; participants encountered in the figure of Abraham the fact that scripture is lively. In other words, the contemporary meanings of Abraham are being sorted out in an ongoing fashion in the homiletical narratives of all three faith traditions, making Abraham a figure who symbolizes richer meanings and yet more elusive than ever.

The final section of the syllabus, *evaluation*, was a reflection of the students' responses to the course's objectives.

Engaging Sermonic Stories: Rhetorical Revelations

To give shape to probing the questions that emerged from the course materials and interactions, I will follow the results yielded by the course's methodology, which entailed the use of classical rhetoric for text analysis.

As a methodology applied to sermon analysis, classical rhetoric proved to be a useful (often new) tool for students and offered a generally level playing field in approaching sermonic material in an unbiased manner. While certainly not value free, rhetorical sermonic analysis did allow for revealing basic suppositions and narrative structures that have formed all three of the homiletical narratives of the faiths studied.

Since preaching and rhetoric have been historically closely aligned, we used Aristotelian rhetoric and the three "proofs" framework as an analytical tool for assessing preaching.[3] Homiletically adopted, the three proofs are:

Logos (the function of words used in preaching and sacred
    scriptures);
Ethos (the role and character of the preacher);
Pathos (the function and responses of the listeners).

This is an artificial separation of components to the extent
that each of the three dynamics is highly interactive with the
other two. All, however, yielded insights and questions for our
coursework as they provided a means of probing the impact of
homiletical narratives in the Abrahamic faith family. In looking at each of these dynamics, the intention was to examine
both the specific sermons studied, and the major questions the
proofs prompted, specifically their ramifications for preaching
Christian faith narratives.

Logos

The homiletical narratives of the Abrahamic faith family all
have some relationship to their respective sacred scriptures.
As a result, course participants looked at two major areas of
discourse: first, the sacred scriptures of the three Abrahamic
faith communities and, second, examples of their sermons,
which may or may not have been based on scriptural passages.
In the process of rhetorically analyzing the printed and spoken word, students were asked to address issues of intentionality, language use, and sermon forms inasmuch as they could
determine them.

The three sacred scriptures of the course—Hebrew, Christian, and Muslim—were introduced with the assumption
that everyone had read the first two. For most students, the
"big event" was the opportunity to read the Qur'an. Reading
the Qur'an put class participants in a new religious neighborhood, one with only a fleeting resemblance to the Judeo-Chris-
tian scriptural universe to which they were accustomed. New
vocabulary; a different way of speaking about recognizable

figures; another scriptural language to look at; and, above all else, a way of thinking, relating, and speaking about God. Class participants' experience was, in general, that of meeting an opaque work that both frustrated and encouraged them to delve more deeply into the Qur'an and commentaries on it.

Most important, with this comparative scriptural approach, students were forced to ask how they were reading and preaching Christian narrative within the contemporary national and international presence of other sacred scriptures. While only a small amount of time was spent on this particular course objective, students had the opportunity to look at the lectionary cycles typical of Hebrew and Christian scriptures and at the use of a reading cycle for the Qur'an that can be completed during the month of Ramadan.

Given the global framing of sacred scriptures today—both through the lectionary and in the public square—media accounts of the last ten years have reasonably demonstrated that all sorts of sacred scriptures govern human action. Decisions great and small are made—and reported on—based on scriptural warrants. Whether land is being claimed (legally or illegally), lives built up or destroyed, pilgrimages undertaken, conversions made, religious practices discussed, bombs thrown or peace gratefully made, politicians overthrown or elected, a naive reading of the Bible in isolation from knowledge of other sacred scriptures is no longer a feasible approach.

Throughout our discussions it was evident that our narrative homiletical work must take into consideration the "neighborhood of sacred scriptures" in which a specifically Christian reading and proclamation takes place. The listeners to our Christian homiletical narratives are no longer just those in the pews and our narrative claims are no longer assessed only by those who are fellow Christians.

This cross-tradition read of all three scriptures raised more questions: Does a Christian homiletical narrative have a privileged place anymore? And if it does not, how are we Christian preachers to regard it as a voice in religious life? If we quote the Hebrew scripture in our Christian preaching, can we also quote the Qur'an? (This latter question was raised by the fact that a handful of students did just that over time in our seminary corporate worship setting as well as preaching class). If I am more knowledgeable about my neighbor's sacred scripture—one not my own—what does this mean for my life in community and for how I answer the question, "Who is my neighbor?"

A second area of rhetorical analysis related to logos was the work students did with sermons from each of the three faith traditions. Sermons were garnered from a number of websites, which included those of religious communities, seminaries, and educational sites. Some used sermons from printed collections and in a couple of cases students received unpublished sermon manuscripts from preachers.

What did these sermons have in common? Class participants had a deeply touching realization that those who spoke the words of the various sermons, from all the traditions, were intent on forming the faith lives of their listeners. Much of the preaching—in various mixes—conveyed a sense of passion, justice, pastoral care, encouragement, and the preacher's sensitivity to the listeners' context within the greater concerns and views of the given faith community. A female rabbi in California, a Muslim preacher in Michigan, and a Christian preacher in Washington were similar in expressing their narrative care for listeners.

Some sermons also presented cultural and religious narrative barriers to the students. In some Jewish and Muslim sermons, the divide between East and West was emphasized, leaving students with an unexpected outsider feeling. Other sermons talked about festivals and rituals foreign to Christians or celebrated in radically different ways with completely different interpretive grids—such as Passover. In several instances, references were made to religious realities and texts about which all of us were clueless. One rabbi's sermon on the

Sabbath contained a reference to the law, which puzzled us. He was kind enough to clarify what he meant when we contacted him through his synagogue's website.[4]

While one could not easily transfer one sermon into another faith's pulpit, a recognizable and consistent homiletical thread was evident, uniting most of the sermons in faithfulness to a religious metanarrative to which the preacher was inviting and urging the listeners. This insight led back to the same question again: What is special about the Christian narrative expressed in preaching? What about scripture and our homiletical words is unique and what is generally similar to others in the Abrahamic faith family?

Ethos

The second proof of rhetorical analysis addresses the person of the contemporary preacher. The term *ethos* is used in the older, classical sense of the preacher's character. The older parts of this tradition also assume that a good character yields a genuine preacher, although obviously persona may be assumed and may mask bad intentions.

Inasmuch as we could glean any information about a preacher beyond the sermon itself, we also attempted to trace his or her influence and intentions in the sermons studied. This venture proved fruitful and at other times limited, since information about the preacher was often lacking: the nature of the preacher could only be traced through attempting to discern the nature of the intentions rendered in the sermonic text. In other cases, if sufficient numbers of sermons were available in print or on websites from the same preacher, the class could form a clearer idea of the preacher's character.

In the matter of ethos, the class was able to discern most clearly what can be described as pastoral care exhibited in the leadership role of preaching. Here similarities among the traditions were most prevalent and valued. Whether one is a rabbi, a Christian preacher, or an imam, one and all must seek solitude, sit alone, think about the listeners, consult the texts, write, and pray that what is written and delivered is the best that homiletical narrative leadership can produce in the given context. The influence of ethos in the sermons was derived above all else from the expectations of what each Abrahamic faith community deems to be a sermon. In all three cases, the prescribed tradition of the sermon form significantly affected the range of choices for any preacher. Islamic preaching, for example, has a two-tiered sermon form inherent in the tradition. Christian preaching is wide ranging but rarely without reference to the Bible. Jewish preaching also showed allegiance to discussing major festivals such as Yom Kippur. In other words, while the preacher had great freedom to speak, not all forms constitute options from which to choose. Preachers are not free-range creatures!

Sermons invariably present themselves as the words of a religious leader. If narrative leadership is demonstrated in the act of preaching, what evidences of that did we extrapolate from the sermons we studied? The following elements repeated themselves throughout the large corpus of sermons we read or listened to:

- Faithfulness to a tradition's allowable or designated sermonic forms; in other words, the preacher's ethos is linguistically boundaried
- A sense of the preacher's role in extending the particular religious tradition
- Encouraging people to stay the religious course
- Alerting listeners to dangers or obstacles
- Narrative freedom to chide and admonish listeners if deemed necessary
- Teaching listeners concepts, ideas, or actions that will enhance and maintain faith
- Using various types of stories to buttress faith claims; these stories may or may not be based on scriptural, traditional, and contemporary sources

+ Charting possible faith responses that may or may not
  be approved by "the world"
+ Speaking consistently about the fact that judgment will
  be rendered on the listener's life of faith, actions, and
  choices

Class participants also found that the analysis of preacherly
ethos is directly connected to evidence of faithful living in the
preacher, whatever her or his religious tradition. They also observed that the characteristics of holiness and faithfulness in
preachers are not peculiar to the Christian tradition. The response of one participant on hearing the live sermon of a long-
time imam was, "He is radically different from what I know
to be the 'flamethrowers.'" A pastor said of the same overall
worship event in the mosque, "I experienced God there and I
am not sure as a Christian what to do with that response." In
summary, the rhetorical analysis of ethos in the preaching of
the three traditions raised other categories to consider, such as
witness, faithfulness, and leading a holy life.

Pathos

The third rhetorical dynamic is pathos, or the presence and responses of the listeners to the preacher and the preacher's words.
Two factors figured largely in this discussion. First, we the class
had become the object of our own studies. The question for everyone with each sermon we studied was: How am I affected by
this sermon? Second, because the congregational context was
largely unknown, we could only guess at the type of listeners to
which the sermons were directed. Occasional printed or website
descriptions of the congregations proved helpful.

The analysis of audience presence and interactions includes
assessing who is not present as a listener. One of John Chryso-
stom's sermons scolds the small congregation present one Sunday because other parishioners were attending horse races at

the Hippodrome. Did he hope his homiletical wrath would get back to those who needed it, giving them a sermon even if they were absent? In some cases, we wondered if we were the absent-yet-addressed of a given sermon.

After some analysis of the dynamic of pathos, it became evident that its boundaries were further extended by asking if there were intended audiences beyond those in a given faith community. Some sermons on the Internet seemed to have as their audience the global community of both adherents to and challengers of their faith tradition. These sermons were in some sense generic but also specifically focused on promoting the faith tradition to both believers and nonbelievers. Other sermons also seemed in dialogue with or in direct opposition to audiences within their own tradition with whom the preachers disagreed. Listeners, in any case, were taken seriously and, in general, treated linguistically as those who had a right to expect and to hear a word from or of God for their lives.

Envisioning the Narrative Future: Educational Strategies for Interreligious Comparative Homiletics

The January course revealed several factors and prompted other questions beyond the field of Christian homiletics. It became evident to me in designing the course that the area of interreligious homiletics is new. Others have yet to probe the exciting possibilities for designing such a course or variants of it; this essay serves as an invitation to those professionally placed in the field of homiletics to explore this avenue for enhancing and contextualizing Christian faith narratives as pedagogical strategies for developing narrative leadership. The venture calls for risk taking and collaboration across several fields of scholarly endeavor, including systematic theology, world religions, and biblical studies. Efforts can also bring into view new human and communal relationships that cut across traditional denominational and faith boundaries.

For any instructor embarking on such a course, identifying and collecting the primary narratives, which include sacred scriptures and selected sermons, is crucial. This collection of resources will proffer two questions immediately: How do we preachers regard our Bible stories, some of which are also contained in various fashions in the sacred scriptures of other religions? In viewing the Bible within a neighborhood of scriptures, does that affect who we speak of in our contemporary preaching narratives?

The first question pushes people to see that the biblical narratives have horizons that supersede the written page. This can be both threatening and life giving in that God's presence and actions may be seen to radiate throughout a much larger human community of godly storytellers than one might have first imagined. This strategy does not necessarily entail agreement with other versions of faith stories but recognition of the mysteries of God's work in the lives of others and their resultant narratives. During our week together, course participants increasingly reflected on how the narrative materials of the "others'" traditions made them rethink the nature of the God they love and worship.

Second, how then might our preaching narratives be affected by shifting scriptural contexts? This is not merely a matter of the historical biblical record or even the sacred scriptural records of different religions. It is also an issue of struggling with the core question, "Who is my neighbor—today?" and finding ways to articulate that in interreligious terms based on biblical narratives recounted in our preaching. This question must be asked if our proclamation is to have any integrity within the global, pluralistic milieu that is our world today. This challenge unfolded for the class and remained as a challenge to all its preachers at the course's conclusion. The enigmatic and problematic nature of the questions is well summed up by Steve

Prothero, professor of religious studies at Boston University: "Moreover, we may be at a tipping point where we are realizing that you cannot really respect a religion that you do not understand and that understanding a foreign religious tradition means wrestling with ways in which that religion is fundamentally different from your own."[5]

Prothero's words were repeatedly reinforced as class participants encountered that which seemed identical or at least similar to our biblical narratives and yet often simultaneously left us on the cusp of meeting the radically different. Immersion in the sacred texts of three faiths and their verbal offshoots—sermons—brought us back again and again to asking, Who is God? Who is my neighbor? Just as the questioner stood before Jesus and asked which commandment was the most important, the course sharply reminded us that, in our struggle with these two realities and their interconnections, answers and reflections were demanded of us as well.

In reflecting specifically on the course's ramifications for the weekly work and act of preaching, three issues emerged and followed us out the door, so to speak. First, *biblically*, what is to be gained by speaking our faith with a consciousness of the multiple religious contexts in which our domestic and global cultures find themselves? This question puts both preacher and listeners on the line between proclaiming the uniqueness of their faith narratives and living in community with those who profess other religious narratives. The question inevitably also raises the adjacent issue of what it means to do evangelism and why. This question has no single answer, but a thoughtful range of responses can be developed by individuals, religious leadership, and faith communities. Certainly, one initial response is a willingness to become familiar with the sacred scriptures and sermonic forms of other religions' pulpits.

Second, course participants identified one major value of the January course as locating the homiletical narrative work of the religious leader in contexts that extend beyond the sermon itself; this homiletical narrative work is an ongoing process. For example, how might preaching narratives that attempt to draw Christianity into the daily narrative marketplace affect the discourse, choices, and programs of a congregation and individual parishioners each week? Students recognized the work to be done in placing their homiletical narratives within the social and global metanarratives in which they and their listeners live.

Finally—and perhaps most important—reading, discussing, preaching, and thinking about interreligious scriptures and sermons led to personal encounters. Some encounters were brief while others were more extended. Through the process of the course and beyond it, the governing category of the *other* shifted in some cases to the *neighbor* and beyond that to *friend*. One pastor living in a remote area of Pennsylvania reported that after the course he made friends with a young rabbi in his area. Together they read scripture and support one another in the daily work of ministry.

Undoubtedly, this pioneering course offered the beginnings of models of contextualization for Christians seeking ways to relate their preaching and their daily lives more lovingly and thoughtfully into the fabric of the cultures they inhabit. While much work remains to be done in the multiple areas the course engaged, the motive for doing so is undergirded by the invitation of the tantalizing final verse of John's Gospel. The writer describes the possibilities of adventuring into the stories of our faith narratives beyond anything we might imagine! "But there are also many other things that Jesus did; if every one of them were written down, I suppose that the world itself could not contain the books that would be written" (21:25).

Notes

~

Nassim Nicholas Taleb, *The Black Swan: The Impact of the Highly Improbable* (Random House: New York), 2007, xviii.

1. On the final day of the course, the class attended the central Friday worship service at the Islamic Center on Massachusetts Avenue in Washington, D. C. We are indebted to imam and preacher of the mosque, Dr. Abdullah M. Khouj for sharing a meal and his thoughts with us that day.

2. For the latest editions of these works, consult a library or the Internet. Also note that any Qur'an in a language other than classical Arabic is not considered—strictly speaking—the Qur'an. The work cited contains both the Arabic and English translation.

3. The quote from Aristotle reads: "(ii) Rhetoric may be defined as the faculty of discerning the possible means of persuasion in each particular case. These consist of proofs, which are (1) inartificial (see xv); (2) artificial. The latter are of three kinds: (1) ethical, derived from the moral character of the speaker; (2) emotional, the object of which is to put the hearer into a certain frame of mind; (3) logical, contained in the speech itself when a real or apparent truth is demonstrated." Aristotle, *The "Art" of Rhetoric*, trans. John Henry Freese (Cambridge, MA: Harvard University Press, 1982), xxxvi.

4. Thanks to Rabbi David Lister of Muswell Hill Synagogue, London, England, for his response to our class. We used a sermon of his, which was archived on a website of Hebrew Union College, Cleveland, Ohio.

5. Stephen Prothero, *Religious Literacy: What Every American Needs To Know—And Doesn't* (San Francisco: HarperSanFrancisco, 2007), 121.

CHAPTER 4

Enlivening Local Stories through Pastoral Ethnography

~

MARY CLARK MOSCHELLA

M any pastors are good listeners. They know how to open up a conversation and invite people to share the pain, struggles, and signs of growth in their lives, yet often pastors stop there and fail to help members of the congregation form a collective story of where the people of God are being led. Ethnography is a structured method of participant observation of group life that equips pastors to listen more carefully and intentionally to the collective stories of a faith community.

As a research method, ethnography opens a door through which deep stories emerge: personal stories, communal stories, faith stories. Stories have the power to calm and comfort as well as the power to disturb and disrupt life as usual. Biblical stories, of course, do both. Pastoral ethnography is a practice that can enliven the stories people and congregations tell and open the way for creative improvisation as a community composes the future chapters of its shared life.

I have been teaching ethnography as a pastoral practice to students of ministry at the master's and doctor of ministry level for more than eight years. Pastoral ethnography takes the methods of qualitative research and congregational studies and presses them into pastoral theological service.[1] When pastors or rabbis conduct ethnographic research in their ministry settings, the power of storytelling and pastoral listening whirl together. The resulting frappe is not exactly a smoothie but often a heady mix of honesty and new revelations, invigorating relationships previously hampered by too much posturing and pretending.

My primary field is pastoral theology, a particular form (rather than a branch) of theology closely related to practical theology.[2] Pastoral theology has historically emphasized the human life cycle and human personality, which has led to a great deal of seminary teaching in pastoral care and counseling. In the last thirty-five years or so, due to the influence of liberation theologies and the intellectual trend of postmodernism, the paradigms for pastoral theology have shifted considerably.[3] Very broadly speaking, these shifts have been away from an exclusive focus on care and counseling for the individual—the one lost sheep who has gone astray—and toward considerably more communal and contextual models of care. Wider lenses bring into view the flock *qua* flock—the ninety-nine left on the hillside as well as the conditions of the hillside, the neighboring environs, and the wider world—what Bonnie Miller-McLemore has called the "living human web."[4] This model gives rise to such questions as, how can a religious leader intelligently care for the whole congregation and the wider community of which it is a part? And, how can congregations themselves begin to respond in more faithful and prophetic ways to the "living human web[s]" both within and beyond the local group?

I see ethnography as a method—a pastoral practice in and of itself—through which theologians and pastoral leaders can live into this communal, contextual model. Ethnography can give religious leaders ears to hear their people's own deep wisdom and longing for God. This research can be a form of pastoral listening to a congregation, community, or group—listening that promotes deep and rich theological conversation, listening that leads to spiritual transformation at the level of praxis.[5] Researcher Lynn Davidman argues that "the telling of lives always changes those lives."[6] In recent years ethnographers and anthropologists have come to terms with the realization that social research does affect research subjects and that it also affects researchers. Social researchers are not neutral observers who can capture an objective and static picture of group life without disturbing anything. Rather, they are active participants in research relationships with real human persons.

These realizations have increased the workload in these fields as scholars have had to address both the increasingly complex epistemological issues in the production of knowledge—a sort of social-science uncertainty principle—and the increasingly intricate ethical issues in the conduct of research and writing. The ethics include issues of power and respect in relationships with research participants, issues of permission and informed consent, and issues of authority and control over the ethnographic narrative, with the concomitant danger of subtle forms of colonialism in the characterization of cultures.

Qualitative research changes lives. This awareness makes all social researchers' work more complex, but it also makes it more theologically compelling. As it happens, pastoral and practical theologians have been interested in the telling of lives and the changing of lives for a long time. Over the years, a number of different metaphors have been used to describe a connection between speaking, listening, and personal and communal change. Terms such as *healing* (Seward Hiltner); *growth* (Howard Clinebell); and more recently, *emancipatory praxis* (Brita Gill-Austern); *liberation* (Carroll Watkins Ali); and *resisting* and *empowering* (Bonnie Miller-McLemore) all point to the pastoral function of promoting spiritual growth.[7] Certainly, scholars and practitioners in the more specific area of pastoral counseling have understood that the process of telling one's story and being well heard can bring change, healing, and hope.[8] When a person tells his or her story to a careful listener, something shifts for the teller. In the best case, the speaker experiences insight; subjectivity is enlarged. "Hearing [someone] to speech," in theologian Nelle Morton's famous phrase, is a profoundly life-giving activity.[9]

I teach ethnography as a pastoral practice that is analogous to individual pastoral listening. Theologians and pastors can help "hear to speech" both the individual and collective voices that emerge through the ethnographic research. This approach elicits complex sociocultural narratives of congregations and communities and honors differences as well as shared meanings and practices. Most critically, this is a method for nurturing emerging theological insights and practices that promote social justice within the community and beyond it. Ethnography is a form of "emancipatory praxis" that can spark theological growth and change.[10]

As may be evident already, this approach relies heavily upon the extensive body of literature in the fields of congregational studies and sociology of religion. I collaborate with these disciplines while also offering some slight shifts in focus. The first such shift involves keeping the focus on pastoral theology throughout the entire research process. From the early stages of research design, I encourage students to identify their own theological positions on the questions and the religious practices they choose to study. For example, often I discern a theologically inflected theory along the lines of "What's wrong with this church?" that motivates a pastor or student intern to want to learn more.

Identifying the researcher's theology, purpose, and hopes for the group is a critical part of this work. This reflection on one's own role in the research is what ethnographers call "reflexivity" or "positionality."[11] The practice of reflexivity requires the pastor-researcher to try to know and articulate his or her own personal, pastoral, and theological motivations behind the research question. This theological self-awareness is cultivated throughout the research, analysis, and writing processes.

For example, in the analysis and writing phases of the work, students are encouraged to ask questions such as, "Where is God in this setting?" or "Where is God in this story?" Even when studying a seemingly bleak community, such as a dying congregation or a mean-spirited one, the class comes back to these questions. It is a way of asking student researchers, "What do you see here of God?" or "Where do you witness hope in this setting?" Reflections on biblical and theological values are invited and investigated. As pastoral ethnographers construct their narratives about the corporate life of the group, they are reaching toward the larger reality, generating hope. As pastoral theologians Herbert Anderson and Edward Foley put it, "storytelling is an act of hope, and even defiance, because it carries within it the power to change."[12] Composing these narratives is a way of invoking the change we seek, a fundamentally theological endeavor.

Along with being a more consciously *theological* endeavor, ethnography as a pastoral practice is also a more consciously *pastoral* activity. Surveys are not conducted merely to gain information (or to test customer satisfaction, heaven forbid!). The goal of the research is to increase one's understanding of people's particular values and longing for God; this includes their "deliberative theology," which may be directly discussed, as well as their "embedded theology," which is revealed through story or practice.[13] The research is conducted to deepen relationships between and among researchers and research participants and to enhance the quality of theological conversation and liberative practice among members of the community.

Pastors and rabbis are good candidates for this work. They occupy a kind of liminal social space that is not so far away from the role of participant-observer.[14] A pastor's function requires both closeness and distance from the group. If, with informed consent, a pastor or religious leader can step back a bit into the role of a pastoral researcher, then the asking of questions and the telling of lives that results can have a profoundly deepening effect on the pastor's relationship to the people. Through this process, new knowledge is uncovered or generated, along with the new experience of telling and hearing and being heard.

To be clear, as practical theologians John Swinton and Harriet Mowat point out, interviewing is not counseling, and I am not suggesting it should be.[15] Yet, interviewing is not mechanical. It involves live relationships and the possibility that shared wisdom might emerge.[16] This requires reverence. *Care-full* tending of pastoral relationships during the research process allows for this potential opening for mutual spiritual growth.

The second slight shift in approaching ethnography as a pastoral practice is toward a greater focus on what is done with the results of the research. I view sharing the findings with the congregation or group as having crucial significance; using the analogy of pastoral listening, this is the reflective listening phase of the pastoral conversation.[17] In an individual pastoral counseling conversation, a pastor might repeat or paraphrase a congregant's words, reflecting them back to the speaker both for the sake of clarification and to validate or magnify what the congregant has said. The experience of hearing one's own words and ideas reflected back to one is often salutary; this has been evidenced in work with groups as well as individuals.[18]

The pastoral ethnographer pieces together a narrative and offers it back to the group for the sake of clarification and validation, as if to say, "This is what I hear you saying. Have I got that right?" The ethnographic narrative will always be biased and limited, but ideally it is the researcher's honest and rigorous portrayal of the congregation's larger story. The congregation then responds. In the back and forth of listening and hearing and testing and negotiating the interpretation of shared symbols and practices, the community's real values, both embedded and explicit, are expressed and made available for reflection and revision. This dialogical process can open up a deeper level of honest conversation and relationship within the community, thereby sowing seeds for transformation.[19]

I have been privileged to read about how these dynamics play out in the ethnographic studies my students have conducted. These local studies address such topics as race, church growth, multiculturalism, and the relationship between spiritual practices and social justice work. Students have conducted their studies in diverse contexts of ministry, including congregations, youth groups, denominational agencies, nursing homes, retirement communities, hospice groups, theological schools, and college dormitories, among others. They have listened to the stories of Hmong immigrants, of the wives of Korean students, of church members engaged in cooperative ministries, and of pastors in cross-racial or cross-cultural ministry appointments.

These projects have usually involved the pastoral researcher asking the members of his or her group a few simple questions in an effort to better understand a particular religious practice. These questions may be offered through a survey or an interview or in a focus group setting. When such honest questions are offered in a spirit of curiosity, people are often willing to answer forthrightly. Indeed, people are often grateful to have a chance to tell their stories, especially to an attentive listener. Given that pastors are sometimes perceived as judgmental or morally authoritative, the stance of a researcher can provide a pastor with a less charged role. If the questions are open ended, and the pastor is nonjudgmental and nonargumentative, he or she will usually learn something new. Even though some respondents will tend to be circumspect, and even though some will lie, an observant pastor-researcher will be rewarded with much helpful information.

By adopting ethnography, the pastor becomes a learner who can better read the shared knowledge and habits that constitute what some authors call "the culture of the congregation."[20] By observing religious practices, the social interactions that comprise and surround them, and the material aspects of the group's communal life—its art, artifacts, architecture, and landscapes—the pastor-researcher adds substance and data to the ethnographic narrative being constructed.[21] Thus the practice of research can become a form of holistic pastoral listening that attends to the range of meanings, experiences, desires, and theologies that people express through diverse idioms.

Teaching Pastoral Ethnography

Teaching pastoral ethnography is best accomplished by assigning students an actual ethnographic study that they conduct as they are reading about the process. When my students engage in research projects in their local ministry settings, they are often surprised. Many come to this task reluctant and afraid. "I approached the group with my request for interviews with some trepidation," one student wrote. "Would they even agree to the project? Would they perceive it as a violation of privacy or meddling? Would they be reluctant to sign a formal document such as a consent form?"[22] This doctor of ministry student, Janice Trammell-Savin, is an interim ministry specialist who used her study to probe the experience of her current congregation's search committee members. She had a hunch that the members of such committees often experienced spiritual growth through their shared service to the congregation. She happened to be serving a church where the search committee had just completed its task and a new pastor was soon to be installed. Because these committees usually operate with a high degree of confidentiality, Jan was particularly concerned that the members might not want to talk with her at all. Though she emphasized to the members that she would interview them only about the search process and would not ask anything about particular candidates, she was still anxious because often an unspoken hands-off rule dictates that interim ministers not try to influence the search process. In spite of her trepidation, knowing she needed to fulfill her assignment, Jan bravely approached the committee members to see if they would consider being interviewed.

As is often the case, the experience of the ethnographic encounter is what teaches. Members of the search committee did agree to be interviewed, and they later told Jan that the interviews she conducted had been highly valuable to them. The interviews gave committee members an opportunity to reflect on the spiritual aspects of the search committee experience, a chance to tell their stories. This telling of lives helped the members name and solidify the spiritual growth they had experienced through serving on their pastoral search committee. The members told stories of struggle and doubt and coming close to quitting their work on the search committee, yet finding strength in one another. In listening to these stories, Jan was deeply moved. She interpreted the life and growth of the committee as "the body of Christ in microcosm, and what the entire church might be like at its best."[23]

One of the pastoral theological implications of Jan's ethnographic work was that she began to reimagine the role of an interim pastor as one that includes providing some kind of debriefing opportunity for search committee members. Indeed, pastoral search committees, because they usually operate confidentially for the protection of the candidates, often lack a safe space in which they can talk about their difficult work, work upon which the future of the congregation depends. Through her ethnographic project, Jan had discovered a way to provide that safe space without compromising the confidentiality of the candidates. Jan decided to continue to develop this practice of ministry, and may write about it, in order to elucidate its potential for enhancing pastoral care relationships between interim pastors and search committee members.

Teaching pastoral ethnography is also best accomplished through the format of a seminar in which students can teach and learn from each other. This is important for several reasons. For one, the subjective nature of the work and the complexity of managing the dual role of minister and researcher require careful ethical monitoring and peer review. In addition,

seminars allow students try out their ideas, name their theological motivations, review each other's research designs,
and practice interview questions. If in planning the syllabus
enough time is allowed, students can also share their findings
and analyses with each other. This can lead to deep sharing,
where students tell parts of their own stories and share their
own growth in understanding as it emerges over the course of
the term.

Once this research process with peer support gets going,
students do not always want to let it end. After one class continued to meet periodically through a second term, the importance of time for this process to unfold became clearer to me.
In response to this (exceptional) group's pleading, I recently
taught a master's level course in a yearlong, two-semester format (two credits per term). This adjustment follows the logic
of the subject matter. Ethnographers often spend years going
back to a group again and again, in different seasons, in an effort to understand the life of the group more fully. In addition
to the time needed for conducting thorough research, time is
needed for sharing study results with the congregation. The
second semester allows time for the whole experience to simmer: the data boils down to something. Sometimes, halfway
through the process, an ethnographer will come to understand
that he or she was misinterpreting at first. As one student put
it, "What you think you know, may not be what you think it
is."[24] To reach this kind of conclusion takes time.

A third practice integral to teaching pastoral ethnography
is assigning students the task of reading numerous examples of
ethnographic and congregational studies. This gives students
the opportunity to see the ways in which various research
methods can be employed to study religious practices. These
texts also model a variety of ways in which authors choose to
structure their narratives. In one recent class, we covered six
such texts by having two students read each text and present
summaries and analyses to the rest of the class. I try to choose

texts that reflect a good deal of cultural diversity, which is one
of my values in teaching. Students often report that they feel
inspired by reading these studies, which both stimulate theoretical ideas and model practical strategies that students can
adapt for their own purposes.

Effects on Formation

Teaching ethnography to students of ministry can have a dra-
matic effect on their formation. Practicing ethnography requires students to view their congregations or field education
sites as places of learning rather than as practice grounds where
they get to expound upon their newly honed theologies. The
role of a pastoral researcher is a humble one. One student described the experience something like this: "This is hard. I'm all
excited about teaching and preaching; I'm ready for that. And
now I have to hold back on that and ask *them* the questions." In
my view, this is the most important shift a pastoral leader can
make. When students try this, they are often changed, transformed. They come to see themselves and their vocations in a
different light. Students experience a new kind of engagement
with the people they are called to serve. Through the ethnographic encounter, students learn not only *about* the people
they serve but also *from* them.[25]

Ethnography offers students of ministry a chance to engage in what David Mellott, a practical theologian at Lancaster
Seminary, calls "*an act of primary theology.*"[26] Students gain the
experience of respectful listening and honest engagement rather than offering religious leadership as a top-down exercise of
authority over people. A level of mutuality or reciprocity takes
place in this listening, speaking, and sharing process that involves the pastor. This cannot be done in a detached or distant
manner. It requires the pastoral ethnographer to cultivate a

genuine desire to learn. This key shift in pastoral posture is one that often must be tried out to be believed.

In reflecting on this kind of shift in her understanding of ministry, one student wrote:

> I am ashamed to admit that I've "made it" to the level of certified candidate for ordained ministry believing that I could study, consult, and teach congregations without being *affected*. Learning about ethnography and the transformative impact it can have on communities of faith has inspired me to make it the focus of my ministry. This transformation that comes through the humble study and learning together with the community only takes place within the intimacy of faith, trust, and openness. This will never be achieved through a survey or PowerPoint presentation, but rather by my listening authentically with my whole self, emptying myself of the illusion of objectivity, and experiencing as best I can the totality of fears, dreams, hopes, visions, pain, and divine purpose of community life.
>
> I am for the first time frightened of my own call. I am afraid of where this listening, emptying, and experiencing will take me. I recognize that the "secular standards" of success do not apply in this realm. If I continue to rely on those secular standards of practice, I will offer a vacuous ministry. . . . I've learned from ethnography that my challenge is no longer to identify success, but rather evidence of the Spirit at work.[27]

As this student's reflections indicate, pastoral ethnography transforms the researcher as much as the congregation or the community being studied. The research process promotes authentic telling and listening to stories of faith in the midst of the ordinary practice of ministry. When students start to bear witness to the honest sharing of parishioners, they are often surprised and moved and led to imagine a more genuine and *faith-full* pastoral identity.

Pastoral ethnography also influences formation by involving students in an encounter with the social and material dimensions of "lived religion."[28] Examining religious practices from the point of view of ordinary participants, rather than solely from the point of view of privileged elites, is an eye-opening exercise. Social realities that are part and parcel of institutional life come into clearer focus through humble research practices. The presence of social stratification, power struggles, prejudices, and various forms of social inertia may be discovered and explored. Students start to understand these nitty-gritty aspects of congregational life that previously were hidden or mystified by spiritual language. Although the encounter with the mundane and flawed side of faith communities can be painful and at times disturbing, for students to gain this kind of material and historical clarity is ultimately empowering.

Studying a group's actual religious practices focuses students' attention on faith in action, teaching them to begin to "read" the theology and values that are enacted or lived as well as those that are spoken. Apparent contradictions inevitably crop up. These contradictions are ripe areas for study. For example, if the actions of the congregation's governing board don't match the rhetoric of the mission statement, this bears examination. Understanding the way things work, in all of their cultural, temporal, spatial, economic, geographic, and theological complexity, helps students of ministry become wiser leaders, more able to perceive and attune themselves to the values that are embedded in the deep layers of a group's cultural and historical story.

Limitations

One limitation of pastoral ethnography is inherent in any interdisciplinary endeavor: the risk of oversimplifying another field of inquiry. There is the danger of engaging in sloppy or disrespectful borrowing. This is a limit all scholars and teachers come up against whenever attempting interdisciplinary or multiperspectival research and teaching. Because pastoral theology has always been a hybrid field, scholars must read widely across the theological disciplines: theology, ethics, Bible, and religious history are integral to our work. Adding the literature of congregational studies, sociology of religion, ethnography, and examples of religious studies from diverse fields, and then the task of weaving all of these diverse kinds of insight back into a pastoral theological framework, makes the workload challenging for scholar-teachers as well as students. The different starting points of these disciplines and the distinct epistemologies that undergird them must be carefully considered.[29] At the same time, the choice of risking interdisciplinary complexity for the sake of opening up congregational stories may also be viewed as strength.[30] The challenge to integrate different kinds of knowledge and the ability to manage complexity and ambiguity are part and parcel of religious leadership.

A second potential danger or limit inherent in pastoral ethnography is that of role confusion, as the pastoral role and researching role sometimes collide. Practical theologian Thomas Edward Frank describes the story of a parishioner leaning over the pew during a worship service and asking the researcher, "Are you observing today, or are you worshiping with us?"[31] Negotiating ethical boundaries around these roles is a huge challenge. Matters of permission, informed consent, and confidentiality are not simple to teach or to practice.

In any social research, even if the research is conducted well and the researcher has good intentions, the possibility exists that the narratives composed may inflict harm.[32] When we offer back the portrait that we paint, it is always an interpretation; it is a biased, partial, and temporary view. Representations, even if they are accurate, have the potential to startle or confuse as well as empower or liberate. We must take care in the stories we compose and offer back to the congregation, "speaking the truth in love" (Eph. 4:15) and with humility, expecting and facilitating further critique and dialogue. As in any practice of ministry, ethical clarity and accountability are needed, lest the integrity of the ministry collapse.

Opening a Door to Imagination

Pastoral ethnography is an approach to ministry that brings religious leaders into deeper and more honest levels of conversation and connection with the people they serve. Pastoral leaders attune themselves to listening to the stories people tell with their words and with their lives; they try to find the words to piece together a larger story and the courage to offer it back for further comment. The resultant dialogue makes way for honest appraisal of a group's current story and opens the door to intentional coauthorship of its future chapters. Instead of continuing on in endless repetition of what has been done in the past, the group becomes free to reimagine and consciously choose its way.

As Thomas Edward Frank notes, "Participant observation of a congregation's culture is a doorway into its imaginative life. It is also a path into the resources of theological imagination."[33] The tools of ethnography can open a door to the imaginative theological work of a congregation. When this happens, and both pastor and people start to tap in to "the resources of theological imagination," new ideas and energy for change emerge. This approach offers a way for pastoral leaders to harness the power of social research to transform the group's common life and its purposeful work in the world.

Notes

~

1. Portions of this essay are drawn from Mary Clark Moschella, *Ethnography as a Pastoral Practice: An Introduction* (Cleveland: Pilgrim Press, 2008). Used by permission. An earlier draft of this paper was presented to the Association for Practical Theology at the Annual Meeting of the American Academy of Religion on November 18, 2006, in Washington, DC.

2. For a good explanation of the distinction between a branch and a form of theology, see Emmanuel Lartey, "Practical Theology as a Theological Form," in *The Blackwell Reader in Pastoral and Practical Theology*, ed. James Woodward and Stephen Pattison (Oxford, UK, and Malden, MA: Blackwell, 2000), 128–34.

3. For more comprehensive descriptions of these shifts, see Nancy J. Ramsay, ed., *Pastoral Care and Counseling: Redefining the Paradigms* (Nashville: Abingdon Press, 2004) and Bonnie Miller-McLemore and Brita Gill-Austern, eds. *Feminist and Womanist Pastoral Theology* (Nashville: Abingdon Press, 1999).

4. Bonnie J. Miller-McLemore, "The Living Human Web: Pastoral Theology at the Turn of the Century," in *Through the Eyes of Women: Insights for Pastoral Care*, ed. Jeanne Stevenson Moessner (Minneapolis: Fortress Press, 1996), 9–26.

5. Elaine Graham, Heather Walton, and Frances Ward, *Theological Reflection: Methods*, vol. 1 (London: SCM Press, 2005), 170–99. Graham, Walton, and Ward use the phrase "theology in action: praxis" to name the particular method of theological reflection that I draw upon here. My concept of ethnography as a pastoral practice also draws upon another method described in this book, "theology in the vernacular" (200–229). This approach is rooted in Robert Schreiter's influential work on local theology. See Robert J. Schreiter, *Constructing Local Theologies* (Maryknoll, NY: Orbis Books, 1985).

As the double entendre in the title of Elaine Graham's *Transforming Practice* suggests, we, as historical agents, can change or transform our religious practices on the one hand, yet on the other hand religious practices shape us and have the potential to transform us as well. I believe pastoral research that examines religious practices taps into this transformative capacity. Elaine L. Graham, *Transforming Practice: Pastoral Theology in an Age of Uncertainty*, 2nd ed. (Eugene, OR: Wipf and Stock, 2002).

6. Lynn Davidman, author of *Motherloss*, a qualitative study of the impact of motherloss on the subsequent lives of survivors, broaches the subject of the transformative potential of the research process itself in her essay, "Truth, Subjectivity, and Ethnographic Research," in *Personal Knowledge and Beyond: Reshaping the Ethnography of Religion*, ed. James V. Spickard, J. Shawn Landres, and Meredith B. McGuire (New York: New York University Press, 2002), 19; Lynn Davidman, *Motherloss* (Berkeley and Los Angeles: University of California Press, 2000).

7. Seward Hiltner, *Preface to Pastoral Theology* (New York: Abingdon Press, 1958); Howard Clinebell, *Basic Types of Pastoral Care and Counseling: Resources for the Ministry of Healing and Growth*, rev. ed. (Nashville: Abingdon Press, 1984); Brita Gill-Austern writes, "Emancipatory praxis will use whatever tools it has at its disposal to struggle against oppression and to further individual and social transformation," in "Pedagogy Under the Influence of Feminism and Womanism," in Bonnie Miller-McLemore and Brita Gill-Austern, eds. *Feminist and Womanist Pastoral Theology*, 151; Carroll Watkins Ali, *Survival and Liberation: Pastoral Theology in African American Context* (St. Louis: Chalice Press, 1999); Bonnie Miller-McLemore, "Feminist Theory in Pastoral Theology," in Miller-McLemore and Gill-Austern, *Feminist and Womanist Pastoral Theology*, 80. Some of these references are cited in Charles J. Scalise, *Bridging the Gap: Connecting What You Learned in Seminary with What You Find in the Congregation* (Nashville: Abingdon Press, 2003), 78–79.

8. In particular, the work of narrative therapists and pastoral counselors elucidates this dynamic. See Michael White and David Epston, *Narrative Means to Therapeutic Ends* (New York and London: W. W. Norton, 1990). White and Epston highlight the connection between knowledge and power, relying on the work of Michel Foucault. For examples of narrative pastoral approaches, see Christie Cozad Neuger, *Counseling Women: A Narrative, Pastoral Approach* (Minneapolis: Augsburg Fortress, 2001); and Edward P. Wimberly, *Recalling Our Own Stories: Spiritual Renewal for Religious Caregivers* (San Francisco: Jossey-Bass, 1997).

9. Nelle Morton, *The Journey Is Home* (Boston: Beacon Press, 1985). For a more recent reflection on these issues, see Deborah van Deusen Hunsinger, *Pray without Ceasing: Revitalizing Pastoral Care* (Grand Rapids: Wm. B. Eerdmans, 2006).

10. Gill-Austern, "Pedagogy under the Influence," 151.

11. For an explanation of reflexivity, see Hammersley and Atkinson, *Ethnography*, 16–21; on positionality, see D. Soyini Madison, *Critical Ethnography: Method, Ethics, and Performance* (Thousand Oaks, CA, London, and New Delhi: Sage, 2005), 5–14.

12. Herbert Anderson and Edward Foley, *Mighty Stories, Dangerous Rituals: Weaving Together the Human and the Divine* (San Francisco: Jossey-Bass, 1998).

13. Carrie Doehring, *The Practice of Pastoral Care: A Postmodern Approach* (Louisville, KY: Westminster John Knox Press, 2006), 112–18. Doehring borrows the terms *deliberative* and *embedded* from Howard W. Stone and James O. Duke, *How to Think Theologically* (Minneapolis: Fortress Press, 1996).

14. Thomas Edward Frank, *The Soul of the Congregation: An Invitation to Congregational Reflection* (Nashville: Abingdon Press, 2000), 82. Also see Anthony B. Robinson, *Transforming Congregational Culture* (Grand Rapids: Wm. B. Eerdmans, 2003).

15. John Swinton and Harriet Mowat, *Practical Theology and Qualitative Research* (London: SCM Press, 2006), 66.

16. My use of the term *shared wisdom* alludes to Pamela Cooper-White, *Shared Wisdom: Use of the Self in Pastoral Care and Counseling* (Minneapolis: Augsburg Fortress, 2004).

17. For a description of this basic pastoral listening skill, see Charles W. Taylor, *The Skilled Pastor: Counseling as the Practice of Theology* (Minneapolis: Augsburg Fortress, 1991), 34–36. A fascinating discussion of some analogies between learning how to do pastoral counseling and learning how to do qualitative research is found in Eileen Campbell-Reed, "Learning Counseling and Qualitative Research: Epistemological Issues" (unpublished paper, presented to the study group on Religious Practices and Commitment, annual meeting of the Society for Pastoral Theology in Atlanta, GA, June 20, 2004).

18. Mary Field Belenky, Lynne A. Bond, and Jacqueline S. Weinstock, *A Tradition That Has No Name: Nurturing the Development of People, Families, and Communities* (New York: Basic Books, 1997). The authors' landmark work on the "Listening Partners' Project"

involved listening, recording, and transcribing the words of economi-
cally disadvantaged and socially isolated women who met in groups
to talk about their lives. The tapes and transcripts were then given
back to the women to hear or read for themselves. Participants in
this project showed dramatically increased understanding and confidence in their knowledge. Also see the related studies in *Women's
Ways of Knowing: The Development of Self, Voice, and Mind*, Mary
Field Belenky, Blythe McVicker Clinchy, Nancy Rule Goldberger,
and Jill Mattuck Tarule (New York: BasicBooks, 1986 and 1997).

19. Important to this discussion is Don S. Browning's observation that transformation follows the dynamics of dialogue and that
"because it is dialogical, the transformative process is mutual," in *A
Fundamental Practical Theology: Descriptive and Strategic Proposals*
(Minneapolis: Fortress Press, 1991), 279.

20. Frank, *Soul of the Congregation*, 77–100.

21. See Colleen McDannell, "Interpreting Things: Material Culture Studies and American Religion," in *Religion* 21 (1991): 371–87.

22. Janice L. Trammell-Savin, "The Hidden Lives of PNCs" (unpublished paper, Wesley Theological Seminary, Washington, D.C.,
submitted March 9, 2007). Used by permission.

23. Ibid.

24. Terry-Thomas Primer, "Catholics and the Creche" (unpublished paper, Wesley Theological Seminary, Washington, D.C., submitted March 18, 2005), 12. Used by permission.

25. Charles Hallisey makes this distinction. See his "In Defense
of Rather Fragile and Local Achievement: Some Reflections on the
Work of Gurulogomi," in *Religion and Practical Reason*, ed. David
Tracy and Frank Reynolds (Albany: State of New York Press, 1994),
121–62.

26. David Mellott, "Ethnography as Theology: Encountering the
Penitentes of Arroyo Seco, New Mexico" (PhD diss., Emory University, 2005), emphasis in the original. Mellott takes the term *primary
theology* from Aidan Kavanagh, *On Liturgical Theology: The Hale Me-
morial Lectures of Seabury-Western Theological Seminary, 1981* (Collegeville, MN: Liturgical Press, 1984).

27. Michele Van Son, "A Community's Story of New Life
Through Cooperative Ministry" (unpublished paper, Wesley Theological Seminary, Washington, D.C., submitted December 9, 2004),
24. Used by permission.

28. For an explanation of this paradigm, see David D. Hall, ed., introduction to *Lived Religion in America: Toward a History of Practice* (Princeton, NJ: Princeton University Press, 1997), vii–xiii. Also see Jane Maynard, Leonard Hummel, and Mary Clark Moschella, eds., *Pastoral Bearings: Lived Religion and Pastoral Theology* (Lanham, MD: Lexington, forthcoming).

29. For an example of a lucid treatment of these issues, see Swinton and Mowat, *Practical Theology and Qualitative Research*, 3–98.

30. See Lisa M. Hess, "Theological Interdisciplinarity and Religious Leadership," *The Journal of Religious Leadership* 6, no. 1 (Spring 2007).

31. Frank, *Soul of the Congregation*, 63.

32. Madison gives a compelling illustration, in which a documentary film about Ghana was made with the intention of advancing human rights there. The documentary, which focused on one woman's story, actually eclipsed the local Ghanaian people's own human rights efforts and activities. Madison, *Critical Ethnography*, 1–5.

33. Frank, *Soul of the Congregation*, 83.

CHAPTER 5

Shared Narrative

STORY BROKERING AS AN APPROACH
TO CONTEXTUAL LEARNING AT SEMINARY

~

KATHRYN VITALIS HOFFMAN

What would happen if first year seminary students were introduced to narrative leadership by paying close attention to the intersecting stories in their midst? This question began to form in 2004 when I began working as campus pastor and mission leadership coordinator at the Lutheran Theological Seminary at Gettysburg. As campus pastor I had the opportunity to listen to the students' stories through their conversational banter. In my office they explored their hopes and fears of what was happening now that they discerned their call to ministry. Through my work at the seminary, I also attended to the stories of the larger church. As mission leadership coordinator, I helped teach ministerial studies classes; did congregational site visits with students out on yearlong internships; and attended meetings, summits, forums, and all other kinds of gatherings where our denomination, the Evangelical Lutheran Church in America (ELCA), addressed the challenge of preparing missional leaders who are outreach oriented. In and with these conversations were echoes of concern by some seminary faculty regarding the integrity of theological education while addressing the church's concerns. I heard my colleagues ask questions regarding the role of spiritual formation along with the rigors of academic

disciplines of graduate school. Listening to the students, I recognized a longing to make connections between their past experiences and present call, their own spiritual quest and the
theological doctrines, and the realities of the postmodern world
with the institutional church's traditions.[1]

Through my position at the seminary I realized that we were
at a crossroads. In fact, Gettysburg Seminary identifies its mission as "bearing witness at the crossroads of history and hope."[2]
The mission of the church is at a crossroads where the effectiveness of an established institution faces the challenges of doing
ministry in an emerging postmodern culture. I began to see an
opportunity for contextual learning at the seminary by explor-
ing the raw texture of particular life stories as they intersect with
Scripture's stories. For students who normally approach their
ministry with a cabinet categorically filed with thoughts, ideas,
and concepts, I could see their imaginations for ministry being
cultivated by engaging their contexts as story brokers. As the
narratives are thickened, students may also discover themselves
together with the others and the Other in the story, a shared
narrative of God's love for the whole world. To bear witness at
the crossroads of history and hope is to bear witness to the way
God is present and at work by excavating, exposing, and illumi-
nating God's story in the many intersecting stories that emerge
at the crossroads. This calls for narrative leaders.

I developed an integrative contextual learning experience
that engaged seminary students as story brokers for the purpose of learning imaginative approaches for ministry in a postmodern world.[3]

An Overview of the Project

Eight first-year Gettysburg Seminary students participated in
this semester-long learning experience in which each of them

intentionally sought out a place to inhabit outside the church. Through these cultural encounters, the students explored the stories of people who are trying to make ultimate sense of their lives apart from the faith tradition. The contextual learning experience also involved weekly conversations in which the students functioned as story brokers as they integrated these stories with biblical stories, their own personal stories, and the theological doctrines formed within the story of their tradition.

Three Major Components: What, How, and Why

The contextual learning experience (CLE) had three major components—the cultural encounter, story brokering, and imaginative approaches for ministry. These three aspects of the project were incorporated into the methodology to address the what, how, and why of the project.

THE CULTURAL ENCOUNTER

Each of the eight students inhabited a place outside the church in order to be intentionally exposed to the ways people make sense of their lives. We called this component of the CLE "cultural encounters." They occurred about twice a week for three months. Two students attended fitness classes at the YWCA, another went to the local pub, still another spent time at a coffee shop. One student intended to frequent the local diner, but when he couldn't make meaningful connections there, he pursued regular conversation with his cousin, a twentysomething-year-old disconnected from the traditional church and questioning Christianity. One student employed as a housekeeper at a hotel while another one worked as an insurance agent. The eighth student tuned in to the women at the childbirth classes she taught.

STORY BROKERING

While having these cultural encounters, the students were learning how to be story brokers. A story broker is the one who draws out the "multiple narratives that intersect around a concern or opportunity."[4] A story broker *pays attention* to what is happening, *evokes* the stories of what is happening, *listens* carefully to what and how the story is told, *gathers and interlaces* these stories with the biblical story, *discerns* a preferred, emerging story, and *tells that preferred story*. To be a story broker, the student is asked not only to tell the stories but also to broker the stories that he or she hears and experiences. The task is not only to lift up the stories but also to negotiate how these stories find expression.

In the weekly sessions, I facilitated learning as we moved through the different functions of story brokering. Although I planned to focus on each function one at a time, we discovered that they were interconnected and couldn't be easily separated from each other. I developed the contextual learning experience so that the students were engaged as story brokers in the following ways:

First, the students were asked *to pay attention* to postmodern culture. Through individual coaching sessions, the students determined their cultural encounter and identified the ways they would gather stories by paying attention to the specific setting. As students shared their observations, I asked for different perspectives. For example, at our orientation session one of the students shared a story about a homeless woman. He acknowledged his own prejudice of her. He discovered, however, an interesting person once he heard her story. This process of considering different perspectives helped us pay attention to our own mental models or preconceived notions while we engaged our settings as story brokers.

Second, to *evoke* the stories, I had the students explore the types of things that address the ultimate concerns people have regarding their lives. Early on, students tended to categorize the experiences. For example, one student referred to the superficial Catholic who wouldn't think of attending another church. As the student asked more questions of the person, she evoked a thicker narrative that helped her recognize the person's genuine search and difficulty with the irrelevance of some aspects of the tradition.

Third, to *listen* with curiosity and skill, I kept asking more particular questions. When the students were making observations and generalizing about the ways people function, I asked, "What if you simply approached your setting as one interested in human nature?" I encouraged the students to listen as learners and not as caregivers. As the listeners focused on what they were learning rather than trying to determine how they could help, they listened differently. In this CLE, I facilitated an "ongoing inquiry into the generative narratives" that exist in the way people live, move, and have their being.[5] The students not only listened in their cultural encounters but they also listened to themselves and each other again and again as they shared the stories.

Fourth, to *interlace* the stories with a larger narrative, the students were constantly juxtaposing the particular stories from their cultural encounters with the theological concepts they were learning in classes and with the stories they were gathering from their Teaching Parish congregations. As an example, one student engaged in conversation with a woman who was going through menopause and needed to be by the fan for exercise class. The changes she was experiencing related not only to menopause but also to her daughter's life, her physical body, her role as a mother, and how she would connect with her grandson. The story of this "fan lady" and the biblical story of the woman who anointed Jesus's feet shared a narrative of relationships that kept changing over time.

Fifth, to *discern* ways God is present and at work in the cultural encounters, I facilitated an appreciative inquiry of their experiences. Like other aspects of story brokering, this was learned best in ongoing dialogue. A key learning happened about midway through the CLE when an instructor shared his congregation's mission statement and core values. One value identified the church as not being similar to the world. While the entire class was encouraged to get at the soul of the congregation by recognizing its core sense of identity over and against the world, the project's cohort examined the varied story lines to see how the congregation's identity is understood as being both over and against the world *and* interconnected with the world. I encouraged them to recognize the complexity of the ways God is at work in and through the world.

Sixth, to *tell* the story as the preferred story, the students learned to preach as ones who thought in story. One of the students who served on the project's advisory committee led a discussion on the book *Thinking in Story* by a Lutheran pastor and teacher, Richard Jensen.[6] This optional session drew nearly all of the student participants and helped them approach preaching with a new thought process and a way to communicate the gospel in a postliterate culture. The students were also aware that something happens "in the telling." The stories of the sermon do not merely illustrate an idea but "invite participation in the world of the story."[7]

IMAGINATIVE APPROACHES FOR MINISTRY

While the students were engaged as story brokers, they were expected to explore imaginative approaches for ministry. These imaginative approaches were shared by the students through (1) weekly conversations and online dialogues; (2) an essay on congregational leadership; (3) sermons first shared with the CLE cohort, then given to people from their cultural encounters, and finally preached at their field education congregation; (4) a critical analysis of their congregation's theological reflection as it related to cultural realities and its mission; and (5) a final evaluation for the CLE.

An Integrated Learning

The contextual learning experience was developed as an integrative component to the students' 2007 spring semester. Together with advisory committee member and Gospels professor Mark Vitalis Hoffman, the students engaged in an activity we called "story brokering the text" as a ministry application of a Gospel text. Our weekly discussions also corresponded with a half course entitled Integrative Seminar I. This group of eight formed one of four small groups in the class. The CLE cohort, unlike the other groups, integrated the course's content not only with their field experiences in teaching parishes but also with their experiences in their cultural encounters.

The integrated approach I took with this project was enhanced by the eight individuals who served on my advisory committee. Together they were an eclectic group of faculty and staff, students and administrators, lay and ordained, with various levels of church involvement. Our learning was enhanced as they not only advised me but also functioned as coaches to the students, group facilitators, and discussion participants.

Asking the Questions

Throughout the project's implementation, I asked six primary questions. These questions helped me and the advisory committee evaluate the effectiveness of the learning experience and how it was making a difference in the students' formation, learning, and pastoral identity. These questions helped us pay attention not only to the multiple ways that each of the eight students learn but also to the diversity of ways that each one experienced learning. The following questions were addressed throughout the contextual learning experience and the final evaluation:

+ To what extent and in what ways does this contextual learning experience create an awareness of the realities of postmodern culture? What impact do the cultural encounters make on the students' learning? In what ways is the method of story brokering conducive to learning cultural trends?

+   To what extent does the learning approach help students ask questions of their context to help them discern how God is at work in the world?

+   To what extent and in what ways are the cultural stories finding expression in their teaching and preaching? In what ways are the students able to appropriate these stories to their own experience in a way that respects the diversity and otherness of the people who share and participate in the narrative of God's love for the world?

+   To what extent and in what ways does this approach strengthen the students' own sense of call and identity for ministry that engages the culture?

+   In what ways does this learning experience affect spiritual formation? How did this learning experience help the students discern God's presence and guidance in their lives?

+   To what extent and in what specific ways did the students learn imaginative approaches for ministry in a postmodern world?

The Outcome of the Project

The outcome of the project was evaluated through the following means:

+   A review of the discussion notes of the advisory committee meetings

+   A review of the discussion notes from the cohort weekly sessions, the one-on-one coaching sessions, and the small group (in twos or threes) sessions

+ A review of the online dialogues that engaged the cohort and the advisory committee
+ A review of the end-of-year teaching parish evaluations completed by both the pastor-mentor and student. (These evaluations were compared with a sampling of other teaching parish students and with the midyear evaluations completed before the contextual learning experience.)
+ A review of the students' sermons and evaluations
+ A review of the students' essays on ministry as compared to a sampling of other students' essays and the essays they wrote prior to the project
+ A review of the students' midsemester and final evaluation of the contextual learning experience.
+ A review of my notes and reflections through the project

Recognizing Postmodern Realities

The students demonstrated varying degrees of awareness of the postmodern realities as they relate to spirituality. From the stories they gathered, students made the following observations:

"I noticed that spirituality just naturally came up when I simply listened."

"The person I talked to kept asking questions about the church's rules. I think she was really seeking a spiritual connection but just didn't know how to tap into it."

"He was searching for a connection without making a commitment."

"I saw a real distrust of organized religion."

While sitting in a Barnes and Noble bookstore, one student observed the relationship between our engagement with *things* and how this relates to our interactions with others. Through an online discussion she noted:

There were probably about 10 tables taken, either with individuals, couples, or small groups. What really struck me was the number of people who were there alone, working on a laptop or even (old school like me) writing in notebooks. Even among those who were in twos or a bigger group, there always seemed to be a "thing" mediating the interaction: they were looking at laptops, books, magazines or a newspaper, talking to each other infrequently. . . . But they seemed to be more in relationship to the thing than the people. . . . I also noticed very little eye contact at the cafe—people ordering their coffee or whatever always looked up at the menu, then down at their wallets, but rarely at the clerk taking their orders, even though they smiled and said "thank you." . . . So—why do people go to all the trouble of schlepping out to Barnes and Noble?

These observations served as a springboard for further learning about how the realities of postmodern culture are illustrated by the ways we gravitate to our screens. We wondered together about what this means for Christian community and how we communicate.

Recognizing these postmodern realities had the students wondering about truth and how it is known today. Engaged in conversation with a "searching twentysomething who doesn't believe in Christianity," one student claimed that he didn't even know the right questions to ask. "When I was reading my Reformation book, I saw that Luther was trained to lay down the foundations." He then asked a critical question regarding the church's mission in a postmodern world: "If we want to reach out to someone, they may not understand our foundation. . . . How can we reconstruct language, so it communicates to a world where God is irrelevant?"

Keeping It Storied

The students were encouraged to pay attention to the particular stories and remain engaged with the story as an open-ended, not easily resolved plot. For the sake of learning, however, characterizations of the people in the stories were sometimes used to categorize people. For example, while discussing transitions, we referenced our "fan lady," a woman who needed to exercise by the fan because she was going through menopause. People who were on the edges of faith found company with the housekeeper who told one of our students that she believed in Jesus "a little bit." Anyone who has struggled with organized religion was compared to the confused Roman Catholic bride who claimed she wanted the tradition of marriage but without the requirement for annulment if something went wrong. Keeping it storied and allowing the complexity to linger was difficult. As the students became more adept at functioning as story brokers, they didn't jump to abstractions and as a result were able to probe the horizons beyond their own mental models.[8]

Keeping the learning storied meant that the students looked "within a tangled and sometimes confusing maze of intermeshing narratives for clues that may guide interpretation."[9] To keep it storied allowed the students to dwell in the messy middle where the stories' endings were not yet realized. For example, we all pondered the following two stories, recognizing the unfinished story lines and the yet-to-be-developed possibilities for change.

One student shared a story about two women at a bar:

I listened to a conversation at the Livery over the weekend. The conversation was between two women who had not met prior to that day. One woman, who was forty years old, was talking about her children, one of whom was apparently involved with drugs. She was saying how frustrating it is having made many of the same mistakes and having had a brother who died from an overdose. To watch her child do drugs made her feel so helpless. The other woman was instructing her on the type of tough love that she needed to give.

This next story was shared by one of the advisory committee members who, together with her husband, are comanagers at a food bank distribution site:

> We hand out bags of food, and folks also get a chance to choose several items they want from a dry-goods food table. Just being there and seeing people lined up in the cold, some without proper shoes, no jacket, etc., is a scene that is startling enough in this rich—rich for whom, and what does that word mean to each of us, is a whole other point for discussion—society, but one incident stands out. One elderly lady was carefully choosing her five items. We offer everything from large cans of juice and oversized jars of peanut butter to canned meat, etc. She took a small can with no label. She sweetly told me that she thought she'd take a chance on what was inside and that she and her husband would just see what it is. She could have picked something she knew, and yet she did this.

Story Brokering the Text

To meet the requirements for their Gospels class, the students did an integrative project by interlacing the Gospel story with other stories. The students imagined what would happen if a person from their cultural encounter entered the setting of the biblical story. Through the questions we asked, the students explored movies, songs, commercials, and other elements of popular culture as they were juxtaposed with the biblical stories. I noticed several places where the story lines intersected in surprising ways.

One student recognized his mother in the biblical story about the widow at Nain (Luke 7:11–17). This student said:

> What do you say to the mom? I was 16 when my 19-year-old brother died. For four years I was gone too, when it happened I had to just check out. My motto was "whatever" and I could

care less about anything. I was walking through life but I suspended a part of myself. . . . I was not engaged, no direction. Without me being physically absent, I was gone. I guess she lost two sons that day. I was restored to her. I had that turn around moment, that time with God, even as I talk about it I could feel that place I don't want to go. I read a passage in Ezekiel only because it was in [the movie] *Pulp Fiction*. It said, "The soul that sins is the soul that dies." And then, "For I have no pleasure in the death of anyone, says the LORD God. Turn, then, and live" [18:20, 32].

You could have heard a pin drop in that moment. A larger story was brokered in this conversation. As he interlaced his own story with this particular biblical story, identifying his mother's perspective thickened the narrative of his own call story and opened it to new possibilities.

The Gospel stories about Jesus calling people to discipleship intersected with the stories of the bookstore people caught up with their *things*. One student noticed in the biblical stories that "Jesus sometimes distracted people from their 'things'— like the disciples got distracted from their fishing nets, and the woman at the well got distracted from her water-drawing task, and he brought them into relationship with him." This led to such questions as, "Were they so focused on their tasks that they didn't make eye contact with other fishermen or women getting water and didn't necessarily notice the new rabbi on the block?" Or, "Once they saw that *something* that Jesus offered, they were drawn into relationship with him, but would they have necessarily sought him out on their own?"

In the Telling: Preaching the Story

Although the conversations leading up to the sermons were storied and imaginative, the sermons themselves lacked imagination. The preaching itself proved to be challenging and difficult for the students to learn. After the students presented their sermons in class, the advisory committee identified the ways the students used the stories to illustrate concepts but were not yet able to integrate the stories in a narrative form. The sermon evaluations also represented the students' difficulties with preaching and making connections with postmodern experience. For example, one listener wrote in her evaluation, "Today I find myself struggling to get back to church, and from listening to this sermon and after reading it many times through, I can say that I did not get how this portrays God's presence outside of the church."

On the other hand, when the students were sharing stories in weekly conversations or in the online dialogue, we heard the (double) ring of the gospel as a thicker narrative of God's love found expression.[10] While grappling with the faith story of Thomas, the students were encouraged to pay attention to that space between unbelief and belief. As story brokers, they probed that space between the two Sundays, between Jesus's resurrection and his appearance to Thomas a week later. One student concluded, "I guess I saw Thomas as a modern looking for proof. I think he was really a postmodern looking for an experience, a sense of God's presence."

Formed and Shaped by the Story

A pleasant surprise from the project was the strong impact the contextual learning experience had on the students' spiritual formation. Throughout the project, I asked the students to reflect on their own experience. I asked them questions such as, How do you perceive what you are seeing? What is your experience of the experience?

In their final evaluations the students acknowledged their need to deal with the experience of faith as a significant part of learning. The relationship between listening, processing, and living was identified by one student. Another student recognized how her stories intersected with faith issues or biblical passages. Through an online conversation she said, "Specifically, I was struck with the 'intersections' with a text I was working on for a Gospels paper."

One student in particular found this experience to be transformative in his pastoral identity and formation for ministry. "I hate to talk about myself," he began his introduction. "I don't like telling stories. I have no problem writing the term papers in graduate school, but this narrative approach has me frustrated." When the students were sharing their stories from the cultural encounters, he began his by saying, "I don't have anything all that interesting, a conversation I overheard at the coffee shop . . ." He then described an interaction between a woman and a teenaged girl. The other students asked questions and soon he was brokering a story that revealed the complexities of a woman's relationship with a girl who was struggling with a boyfriend's aggression. A few weeks later this student identified the power of narration by describing the movie, *Stranger than Fiction*. He said of the main character, played by Will Ferrell, "He surrenders to the story . . . and gets his life."

He later noted that the "discipleship story intersects with those of us in seminary. I find myself thinking about 'what happens next.' He [the disciple] followed Jesus on the road. How far did he go and where and what else is happening there?" As a story broker, this student discovered that he himself was at a crossroads. He opened up his own call story and began to ask new questions, not only about his own ministry but also about what else is happening in his own experience of following Jesus.

In his final evaluation, this student noted the importance of "providing space and time for the congregation to share their own stories among themselves and also with those outside the congregation." All of this from someone who originally hated telling stories.

Learning Imaginative Approaches for Ministry

This project's intent was to engage students as story brokers so that they could learn imaginative approaches to ministry in a postmodern world. The students learned that *story brokering is in itself an imaginative approach* to ministry. The stories they have heard, shared, retold, entangled, and lived became a way of approaching their call to ministry. One student discovered that he was not called to solve every problem. Another student recognized the possibilities in providing space and time for the congregation to share their own stories among themselves or with those outside the congregation.

Interesting connections were also made between learning and pastoral care. When the students were listening to learn more, they recognized that people experienced it as genuine caring for them. In one instance a student realized that when he functioned as a story broker he refrained from offering platitudes to someone facing difficulty. He commented, "When she started telling me about her cancer, I just asked more questions and listened. I tried to learn more about how this was affecting her whole family and work. The more I listened, the more she talked."

One of the students discovered that emerging stories facilitate emerging ministries. "Go listen, you're likely to be pulled in." He then described the Bible study he is doing at work:

> It just happened. It seemed like the next part of what was happening. It went very well, and it started because of our contextual study project. Apparently while I was listening to stories in my context, my context was watching me. Somewhere along the way I was being pulled into the role of a minister. In the midst of this, I realized that one of the few things I liked about being at work was that it was the only place left where I could be just me. Not that I was really acting any differently than I do anywhere else, but no one had any

expectations of me there in terms of my call to the ministry. Now God has stripped away that hiding place. Does anyone remember this line from *Seinfeld?* "Worlds are colliding Jerry! Worlds are colliding!" That's how I am feeling about hosting a Bible study for my co-workers.

An Interpretation

The final section of this essay offers three glimpses of interpretative reflections. Like many stories that the cohort brokered in this experience, these short pieces are not conclusive as much as they are suggestive. They suggest the possibilities for yet another starting place for contextual learning and explore the experience of contextual learning. The first reflection offers an interpretive analysis of the cohort's and advisory committee's first gathering, the orientation. The second reflection explores the way the participants' understanding of their call to ministry changed through the CLE. The third reflection depicts the implications of their learning for their future ministry in postmodern culture.

A (Dis)Orientation

After accepting the invitation to participate in the contextual learning experience, the eight student participants joined me and the project's advisory committee for an orientation. During this overly ambitious initial session, the students were introduced to the project's purpose, the narrative research approach, and the advisory committee and their active role in the contextual learning experience. The students also joined in a conversation about the postmodern realities that they both experience themselves and recognize in the culture. I evoked several stories that had them juxtaposing a variety of experiences and observations. I shared a children's book that told a familiar story about the three little pigs safely fortressed in their well-built home only to be enticed to explore the world by their younger sister, pig four.[11] From the seminary's ponytailed IT guy, they learned of his interest in Native American spirituality and why he is not into church. A peek into the life and times of the eccentric Elsie Singmaster—a former seminary president's daughter—gave them another story line for Gettysburg Seminary's legacy. With their heads already spinning from the bricolage of learning, I added ringing to their ears with Len Sweet's *Double Ring* video. These are just a few examples of the ways the student participants became oriented to the project and disoriented from seminary education as they knew it.

From Presenting to Presence

The storytellers were gathered in a classroom. They faced each other in a circle. Each had a turn to tell the story. On the third Friday in August 2006, on the first day of summer Greek class, seven of the eight CLE cohort students (one of the students had already fulfilled the Greek requirements) were gathered with the other first year seminary students to tell the story of how they came to seminary. The stories were told well. They were inspiring, most with turnaround plots and heroic characters, all told with smooth transitions and well-developed story lines. They were practiced stories. These descriptions clearly portrayed how a person is convinced to change course, or to continue the course, to seminary. At the time these stories were told, the students had already met with their denominational representatives and had been accepted into the candidacy process. Their stories were ones about the means for entrance into the denomination's formalized call process and then into ministry.

Nine months later on the second Wednesday of May 2007, another set of stories was shared. These eight storytellers were crowded into my office for a spur-of-the-moment gathering.

Actually, one of the cohort members didn't make it to this session; one of the other first year students came along. I shared my appreciation for their participation in the CLE cohort. I gave them each a book—they could choose between a Frederick Buechner or Henri Nouwen devotional—and a candy bar. We laughed about two of my favorite things, stories and chocolate, and how I fed the students with both through the semester. The students shared their appreciation. "It was what I came to seminary for," one said, "to explore these questions." Another said, "There's no cure-all." "The stories I'm hearing are my stories," one noted. There was a spirit in my office. We all seemed to linger with each other and relish the time together. The other student was nodding and smiling as he listened. He said, "I can tell that you are all really in tune and paying attention." We noted the presence of God as we were tuned in together to a larger story with open endings and surprise turns. While we conversed together in that impromptu meeting, I realized that a shift had occurred through the CLE. The students were engaged in what Peter Senge and his colleagues identify as "deeper levels of learning."[12] The students probed the stories that cultivated an "increasing awareness of the larger whole—both as it is and as it is evolving."[13] Here were students who were not simply trying to *get attention* by striving to present themselves well but instead were focused on *paying attention* to the living presence of God.

Hope at the Edges: Where the Stories Intersect

I also noticed that the students became aware of the double-ring effect in postmodern culture. They recognized the ways their ability to be engaged in the culture was strengthened by their ability to keep their learning experiences in tension with each other. The cultural encounter was a key component to opening up the story about ministry. The linear story lines known in their religious tradition were complicated by other story lines from their cultural encounters. These intersecting story lines thickened the narrative of God's presence in the world. The greatest impact was the tension that developed in trying to move the gospel beyond church walls in a way that was relevant and still truth. "That tension," one student noted, "will inform my sermon process."

In this contextual learning experience, we discovered the possibilities that arise at the edges of the stories. We found ourselves paying attention "to the ambiguity at the edge, the permeable border between now and then . . . between self and other."[14] Because of a difference in perspective, we were tuned in differently to God's word.

Unique to this project, I believe, was the freedom to hold the tension in the stories and keep it tight as the edges of human experience were explored. We recognized the importance of countering the impulse for closure with the suggestion of yet another opening. As story brokers, the students became adept at asking particular questions that would evoke more stories. These additional stories would shed light on our earlier observations and change our perspective on an experience. And on the seminary grounds where the battle of Gettysburg had raged, we knew the importance of disarming the polarities of diversity while also savoring the intensity where the edges meet.[15] And here lies hope for the church. Hope is not realized in the foregone conclusion that puts our anxieties at ease. That is not hope, but simply comfort. Hope is discovered as we bump up against our finitude and being surprised, yet again, by the infinite in, with, and under the raw texture of our very lives. This hope finds expression as church leaders broker the stories of God's steadfast love. Narrative leaders, I believe, dwell at the intersections, they linger in the complexity, and they thrive at the edges. This is where they discern the emerging story of God's love for all the world, a shared narrative that bears witness at the crossroads of history and hope.

Notes

1. One student described how his past experience as a firefighter and a bartender are "immeasurably valuable" for his preparation for ministry but finds theological education unable to tap those experiences as they teach only to "one side of the brain."

2. Vision statement, Lutheran Theological Seminary at Gettysburg, October 2000.

3. This project was completed in partial fulfillment of the requirements for the Doctor of Ministry degree at Drew University, Madison, NJ, May 2008.

4. William Presnell and Carl Savage, *Narrative Research in Ministry: A Postmodern Research Approach for Faith Communities* (Muskogee, OK: Indian University Press, 2006), 63.

5. Mark Lau Branson, *Memories, Hopes, and Conversations: Appreciative Inquiry and Congregational Change* (Herndon, VA: Alban Institute, 2004), 111.

6. Richard A. Jensen, *Thinking in Story: Preaching in a Post-literate Age* (Lima, OH: CSS Publishing, 1993).

7. Ibid., 28.

8. Peter M. Senge. *The Fifth Discipline: The Art and Practice of the Learning Organization*, 2nd ed. (New York: Random House, 2006), 163.

9. Presnell and Savage, *Narrative Research in Ministry*, 69.

10. This concept, double ring, has been developed by Leonard Sweet. "Doubleness" is experienced in postmodern culture where reality is experienced in the "dynamic interplay of contraries." See Sweet, *Postmodern Pilgrims: First Century Passion for the 21st Century World* (Nashville: Broadman and Holman, 2000), xviii. See also Sweet, *The Double Ring* video, www.leonardsweet.com/multimedia.php.

11. Teresa Celsi, *The Fourth Little Pig* (Austin, TX: Steck-Vaughn Company, 1990).

12. Peter Senge and others, *Presence: An Exploration of Profound Change in People, Organizations, and Society* (New York: Double Day/Currency, 2004), 11.

13. Ibid.

14. Catherine Keller, *Apocalypse Now and Then: A Feminist Guide to the End of the World* (Boston: Beacon Press, 1996), 133.

15. Ibid., 20.

CHAPTER 6

Story Lines for Redemptive Leadership

~

ROBERT CHARLES ANDERSON

I stumbled upon the concept of narrative redemptive leadership in a writing class taught by Diana Butler Bass of Virginia Theological Seminary. Diana is an advocate of writing our life stories. Her class assignment was for each of us to write a brief story from our real-life experience. I did. It changed my life. It changed my life because the story redeemed a broken part of my soul.

The story was simple. One of my earliest memories is living in East Camden, New Jersey, when I was four years old and visited by a little girl playmate. I retain a vivid memory of the day when she said she needed to leave. Her smile beamed like sunshine, her blue eyes sparkled like a million stars, and she radiated the love only pure innocence and total acceptance can give. She tiptoed up and kissed my cheek while her love and smile entered my soul for life. I watched my little friend climb into a big black automobile. Then she was gone. As a young adult, I asked my mother for the name of the little blond girl who visited me at our little duplex on Rand Street. Mom disavowed knowing any such "little girl."

But my memory never grew dim. When life is tough, I revisit that long ago moment. Writing in my journal one day, I realized that the memory of my childhood friend is a place of peace, security, comfort, and hope in the midst of life turmoil. That day, I named my friend Hope.

A few days before the writing class with Diana Bass, my mother wrote me a birthday letter in which she recalled, without my prompting, that when we lived in East Camden I had an invisible friend, a little girl. She wrote that when we went for walks around the block, I insisted that Mom hold my friend's hand. Mom was on one side and I was on the other. With no one visible in between, we must have made a strange-looking mother and child.

I wrote this for the class exercise and realized that Hope was my invisible friend. Except that on that day, she was not invisible. Hope was my divine gift of peace and hope that entered my soul for life. I told my mother this story and she graciously listened without comment. For other incredulous ones, at least allow that my imagination created Hope as a metaphor for divine trust and hope that has broad redemptive possibilities for my life. I introduced Hope to my writing class colleagues as my friend whom I encountered in a Celtic "thin place" between the eternal and temporal in East Camden. Eternity's veil slipped aside for a brief time and I was kissed by Hope.

Several months after my writing class, I recounted this story to a small group of friends. As I listened to myself tell the story, my heart lit up with the realization that *hope* is my life mission. My call to interim ministry—and the training of interims—is a call to help others discover hope in times of change. For years I tried to write a life mission statement and each attempt was several pages long. This day I practically shouted my epiphany to my friends: "My life mission is to bring hope into the lives of others, and into our world!" Hope kissed me again that day and transformed the ordinary into the extraordinary.

That was a redemptive moment. Redemption is a way of buying something back, winning back, or a repurchase. Redemption is the release or overcoming of something detrimental, or a change for the better. The writing assignment became the catalyst for a journey of life change that continued in the years since. The part of me that was disconnected and broken was redeemed by Hope. I experienced wholeness and was more effective in my life roles. The redemptive moment also affirmed my call to transitional ministry as a ministry of hope. The moment was redemptive because I became a new person and changed for the better. Mostly, I learned that God's love is still actively redeeming life.

This life mission of hope is now wrapped in what I am calling a practice of *narrative redemptive pastoral leadership*. I use the word *narrative* because I believe God uses the stories of our lives for redemptive purposes. This leadership is *redemptive* because its end goal is transformation and new life for the storyteller. The leadership is *pastoral* because the calling is to care for God's people and their souls. Each member of the congregation is a living story yearning to be heard with spiritual care. The practice is *leadership* because the pastor charts the course, practices the craft, mentors apprentices, and serves as the spiritual guide to the richness of redemptive narratives. Redemptive leadership is a practice because it is a skill that can be taught through listening to the narratives embodied in congregational members and their corporate memory. Each telling of the story of God's redemptive love is an opportunity to practice our awareness of God's redeeming activity. And every time we practice telling our own stories to others, we participate in the good news, a story we live through our own stories.

Pastoral leaders who create a safe environment for these stories to unfold form a context for spiritual, moral, and human growth. When I lead interim ministry training, I share my conviction that the practice of narrative redemptive leadership revitalizes our ministerial leaders and transforms congregations.

Our narrative story lines are pathways to the soul of a congregation, for stories shape and form people's lives. I stumbled on the power of this reality when a family member told me

about the stories she once told her toddler son. She related
how she took his little hand, tracing the tiny life lines of his
palm with her fingers. Each became the line of a family story.
He heard about the joyful day he was born, his father's race
cars, his grandfather's home in Ireland, and his new home in
America. He heard the story of how his grandfather worked
several jobs at a time until he could begin his own construction
company. It is no wonder that as a teenager this young man
learned to lay a straight course of block and worked in the family business. Today he is a story-formed man who can trace his
story lines in the palm of his hand.

Practice 1:
The Practice of Tracing Story Lines

As God's people, we are story formed by the stories of our faith
ancestors. Our redemptive story lines are forever etched on
Christ's palm and reflected on ours. Thus, the first practice of
narrative redemptive pastoral leadership is to trace these story
lines across the lives of the people of God and follow them to
the very soul of the congregation.

The soul of a congregation is where God breathes, where the
heart of a congregation beats to the rhythm of God's heart. A
congregation's story will give hints to the pastoral leader about
the deep nature of the congregation's life and mission. Author
Kent Groff has heard the stories of hundreds of congregations
in his Oasis Retreat Ministries. He notes in his book *The Soul
of Tomorrow's Church* that the soul of a congregation is that
place of life where the congregation seeks to actively "re-present
Christ to the world . . . with the integrity, passion, and wholeness of Christ."[1] The soul of the congregation and its story is
inherently missional. The soul of a congregation embodies and
demonstrates the redeeming love of God that gives new starts

in life and makes all things new. The soul of the congregation is the container of its deep story.

Practice 2:
The Practice of Presence

This embodiment or demonstration of God's redeeming love is the core of a second practice of redemptive leadership, the practice of presence.

This practice is the willingness and ability of the pastoral leader to live into her or his life story. This practice involves humility, for to share one's self in story is to get down to earth about one's self. To tell one's story is to become vulnerable. Sharing one's story is to peel back the protective defenses to reveal our authentic selves. The risk can be worth taking, however, for stories are the fundamental ways that human beings connect with one another to form community. Presence is a dynamic awareness of one's self in relation to others that is foundational to being in community.

Harrison is a friend who participated with me in a group story-sharing exercise. Harrison told us that he shared with his listening partner, Terese, the story about how different his life became when he brought home is new dog. Terese, he said, "was a good listener and she noted how I seemed to be creating a family. Until that moment I was not aware of my need for family and community. Terese's comment was like a breeze that blew away a heavy dark cloud as I realized a deep inner need that was haunting me." Harrison had a redemptive moment as Terese listened to his story and helped him probe it for a more authentic self.

The act of telling, listening, and valuing life stories is, I believe, implicitly redemptive. Howard Gardner's study of leaders revealed that effective leaders "told stories . . . about themselves and their groups, about where they were coming from and where they were headed, about what was to be feared, struggled against, and dreamed about."[2] Stories give us a baseline of personal, communal, and divine history that begins to create meaning in our unsettled world. In sharing my own story lines as a pastoral leader, I allow other story lines to weave with mine to create a community of God's story in action, which is a storytelling mission that can provide an authentic presence in the world.

Authentic sharing of one's life story in worship and preaching must be done thoughtfully and appropriately but it can be an effective way of practicing presence.

It was a few minutes before midnight on a summer Saturday when I got a call that my sixteen-year-old daughter, Lacey, had run away with her best girlfriend. Sleep was impossible. I needed to lead worship and preach in the morning. My first move was to ignore it, tough it out, and pretend to be the perfect, problem-free pastor whom I wanted to be and the congregation to see. My spouse's wisdom encouraged me to share the story so that people could pray with me.

I resisted public display to the last moment, preferring to avoid community by living a fairy tale rather than living out of my authentic, real life story. I discovered that my need for community was greater than my need for a fairy tale, however. I took the deep breath of community truth telling and told my story. My story, woven with God's story, became story lines I cast out over the congregation. The congregation grabbed my story lines and wove them into their own. They were captured by my human story in which we all shared. The simple, or in this case, not so simple, act of telling was redemptive. I released my anxious pain into the hands of the congregation. I watched in amazement as their hands were miraculously transformed into Christ's hands.

In a surprising integrative moment, my redemptive story was written by the congregation, not me. They wrote story lines in the journal of my life. They acknowledged my humanity. They described my pain and embraced it. Then they affirmed their love by loving my prodigal daughter when she returned six weeks later to live with Sandy and me. The practice of presence is one of community mutuality. I became present with the congregation and they were present with me. We traced story lines to our souls and together found redemptive, healing balm.

The practice of presence is not easy, however. Generations of seminarians, including mine, were taught that stories about one's self were inappropriate in the pulpit. Some of us are reticent, others prefer to think of faith as a private matter, and others of us are not fully aware of our story lines. I taught some storytelling concepts with a group of Presbyterian ministers recently. The group practiced telling and listening to personal stories. When we processed the experience, no one was surprised that these ministers were skilled listeners. They let me know that my extensive presentation on deep listening was unnecessary. Their startling discovery, however, was their self-confessed acknowledgment that they preferred listening to telling. A consequence was that some of the participants discounted the value of life stories by equating them as sermon illustrations.

My passion is sharing our firsthand accounts of God's life, because stories have a long tradition of forming culture and faith and defining one's place in these worlds. Telling my story as a redemptive leader is not simply about appropriateness or a funny illustration. Nor is it about manipulating people to hear what I want them to hear. The practice of presence is about weaving stories and hearts into a new way of living. That is a theologically missonal outcome. Presence does its work best when, as Gil Rendle writes, the leader "tells a story sufficiently healthy, authentic, and purposeful for others to feel connection, respond with resonance, and find greater meaning. Connection happens when people are able to say to themselves, 'I see myself in that story.'"[3] Pastoral leaders will also see God present in those stories. God's presence redeems our human stories, writing new story lines that prepare us for a new kind of life.

Practice 3:
The Practice of Action-Listening and Reflection

The risks and vulnerabilities faced by the pastoral redemptive leader also confront the congregation. The leader is careful to create safe environments for others to practice telling their stories. Creating a safe place occurs over time as the pastoral leader practices "action listening and reflection."

This practice is a respectful two-part process of active deep or soulful listening and reflecting or mirroring back what listeners heard from the storyteller. Action listening is the art of deep listening on the fly. Many stories are told informally in a brief elevator encounter or on the way out the door on a Sunday morning after worship. *Action* also refers to active listening, a commitment to full engagement with the other. Action listening is a practice that is close to the conscious mind, not easily blindsided by a quick encounter with a redemptive moment, and prepared to shift to full engagement quickly.

Action listening is soulful. The word *soulful* captures a sense of spiritual practice that engages your own soul and imagination. It is a deep commitment to hear the words of another child of God and listen for the human pathos between the lines. As a pastoral leader in congregations and church governing bodies in transition, I find it critical to suspend judgment and set aside my personal references and agendas. I have observed that when I get out of the way, I create empty space for others to grow. The new space allows the congregation to expand their discoveries, to broaden their awareness of what they need to learn, and to increase their capacity for what God is calling them to do and become.

Early in my ministry, a church member commented on the former pastor's habit of snubbing people when they greeted him at the door after worship. She described his manner as "always seeming to look beyond me, scanning the crowd for someone more interesting to talk with." I don't think she had me in mind, but the next Sunday I noticed that I did the same thing. That day I made a commitment to give each person full eye contact and look into their soul with a silent prayer. I did this for several months very intentionally. The result was more stories. Soulful listening and full engagement elicits stories and their redemptive possibilities.

The second part of the process is reflection. This is the well-known skill of mirroring or reflecting back what we heard the other say. In the narrative redemptive context, the pastoral leader mirrors or reflects the story as she or he heard it in word and spirit. I am well known for my responses such as "Tell me more," "What did you do?" or "What happened next?" I also allow silence to do its quiet but creative work.

Anne was an older member of a church where I was a pastor. She traditionally sat in one of the short pews below the choir area. One Sunday I noticed a visiting young couple who sat down with Anne in her pew. Anne appeared perturbed at the intrusion. The next week the couple returned and sat in the same place. Again, Anne scooted over and forced a gracious smile. Shortly after this, Anne was diagnosed with cancer. When I visited her, I asked her to tell me the story about the young couple. She chuckled, saying, "I was so angry when they came and sat in my pew. I almost left." She stopped, I waited in silence for a long, uncomfortable moment. (When I get very uncomfortable and want to say something, I know that is the magic moment for a new story line to bubble up.) With a resolute look she declared, "That's my pew and they should know better." I mirrored back to her that in some way her space was being invaded. "No, not at all, I think they are very nice. But they are sitting in George's (her deceased husband) seat." I made no judgment nor did I try to persuade her differently.

Silence was creating something new. She continued, "Well, how would they know that, anyway? Now that I'm talking about his, I realize George would love it that a young couple was replacing him in church."

Anne traced her story line directly to her soul as God redeemed the memory of her husband's spot in the pew. Redemption also made room for new life in the form of the new couple. Over time, the couple befriended Anne. They were key caregivers during her cancer treatments and hospice program. The practice of listening and reflection created holy ground under my feet and the wonder of it is my burning bush of passion for narrative redemptive leadership.

Practices 4 and 5:
The Practices of Story Weaving
and Re-Storying

The practices of story weaving and re-storying are closely related and, though not sequential or linear, they do inform each other as a story moves to a redemptive future. Story weaving is the practice of creating a coherent whole from a variety of story snippets. Re-storying is the practice of writing a new story after discoveries are made and redemption forms a new way to live. In the practice of ministry, stories are a valuable tool for understanding a congregational system. But often, we encounter plots and themes that don't seem to connect. Others seem related but one is not certain how. Some stories are powerful and enriching. Many stories are snippets that only hint at the larger whole. The process of taking story lines, snippets of stories, or even conflicting stories and gradually creating a coherent narrative is the practice of story weaving. I find it helpful to keep a narrative journal to record the narratives. I can then remember and read, piecing together the various strands of story line, weaving them into a whole. I begin to tell the story back and let the listeners tell me if it resonates with them. When I share the story weaving with others, they can touch the texture of their storied life tapestry and help me to understand the knots, broken threads, and various hues and textures. In hearing their story from me, the interim minister "stranger," they may begin to see themselves differently as well.

Old Riverside was a church where I wove stories, reflected them, became confused, and went at it again. I did that for sixteen months. One day I asked one of the members about a group of locked cabinets near the choir room. Ariel told me that they contained a large and expensive handbell set. "But we don't have a handbell choir," I said. "Tell me about the bells." For the first time I heard that this congregation in its best days had a large music program that attracted people regionally. The bell choir was a key attraction. "We even had music students from the university come to church here and join our choirs because of the music program. We were known as the 'music church,'" Ariel recalled. I kept silence on new holy ground. Eventually Ariel looked at me with moist eyes and wondered, "Do you think we can still be a music church?"

Story weaving traced story lines to a passion laid aside. Ariel began re-storying. The cocoon of twenty years was stirring with the new life, an emergent musical butterfly. Using themes and rhythms of history, a new but related story was emerging. This group began a small bell ensemble and some inactive members returned to play. A previously peripheral member led a song fest with the piano before worship each Sunday. The church called a new pastor who had musical gifts. Later they formed a worship and praise team. It was not the music church of yesteryear, but the story themes were re-storied with hope, and the congregation found their place for a new time. A neglected past was redeemed.

Story weaving and re-storying can be done in a variety of ways. I often use story line techniques with a church's leadership body. I invite the officers to share what the church was like when they joined, how they felt when they were first asked to be an elder, or where they have seen God at work recently. These exchanges deepen relationships and create community.

Including all the members in story weaving and re-storying is also important. I want to experiment with a Church Story Night. I envision a cafe-style setting. Groups would share stories about themselves and the church. They would note key themes on newsprint that cover round tables. Participants would move from table to table celebrating stories recorded, adding notes to some, and writing new ones. The sheets could be summarized for a process of reflection and meaning-making.

Using a congregational time line is a helpful tool. One can be easily created by using a long piece of newsprint with vertical lines that represent ten-year blocks, starting with the founding of the church or the decade in which the oldest member was born. Two horizontal lines separate a section for world events, another for community events, and another for church experiences. The participants add important events in the life of the general community and then important events in the life of the church. Participants tell stories and begin to see where they connect. The time of reflection about creating meaning stretches the group to see themes and patterns. One participant declared, "Well, it sure seems like food is really important to us." Sometimes antagonists appear in the form of ministers. A breakthrough was made by one group when several members made the observation that they seemed to call ministers who abused power. Yet another group made the discovery that none of them were native to that geographical region. They all came from different areas of the country to begin careers. As they listened to the stories shared from the time line, it also became obvious that only a handful had Presbyterian heritage. The group was energized and excited as they uncovered why they were such an "un-Presbyterian Presbyterian church." These accounts are all redemptive at some level. The discoveries allowed God's people to be unstuck, to recover a value from the past, or find the good in a painful experience.

Practice 6:
The Practice of Future Storying

The practice of "future storying" is the process of creating a story about what we want life to be like in the future. Making plans and strategies for the future is often an intimidating list of projects and time lines, endless meetings, and arguments about the best way to proceed. Creating a future story is creative and imaginative. I ask the group I am meeting with to imagine their future in twenty years, using silence and a visualization process. I want to try this with a one-hundred-year look forward. This long vision will focus more on legacy and the spiritual "seeds" that a congregation plants. The task is to write a story about the future they want. Small groups submit their composite story and all are compared for common themes, values, hopes, expectations, and dreams. These elements are included in the plans for the future.

Future stories recognize that words are powerful and creative. Even God is referred to as Word in Scripture. Words are powerful because our Scriptures are constantly ascribing power to words spoken, beginning with God's word that brought and brings all creation into being. Words written are also powerfully creative as we express ourselves. Created in God's image, our *imago dei* has a similar capacity for creating a life and future aligned with God's dreams and desires for us.

My first try at this was a medium-size congregation that gathered as part of the presbytery congregational self-study process. I led the group in a visualization in which they pretended they could hover over the church building in ten years. I then asked guiding questions like, Who do you see? What does the building look like? What does it feel like, smell like? What do you hear? This particular group was extremely imaginative and they created a picture of the future that astounded them.

I encouraged them to create a succinct future story that they could tell others so that with imagination and prayerfulness the vision would emerge as they lived into their future story.

If "faith is the assurance hoped for, the conviction of things not seen" (Heb. 11:1), then the faith-filled people of God will seek imaginatively to bring God's will done in heaven into reality on earth, to paraphrase the Lord's Prayer. The redemptive component is found in creating a future that springs from the people of God as they visualize God's dream and mission for them. The redemptive narrative leader then guides the congregation to live into this new story, a story woven with the strands of generations past and with lots of space for new threads of future generations.

The practices of redemptive leadership are not simply technical program tools. The practices are first of all pastoral because a redemptive possibility exists. Redemptive leaders must tend these practices with theological reflection as well. Most pastoral leadership is practiced in a context of transition, rapid change, loss of the grand framing stories of culture, the demise of congregational stories and a vocabulary for them. The church of today is in a very obvious in-between time. Pastoral leaders are not only involved in theological reflection flowing from narratives, but we are also reflecting eschatologically. This eschatological story work of congregational life and future is not the doomsday "last days" eschatology of some circles, however.

Narrative pastoral redemptive leadership in our age of discontinuity helps us find hope through the redemptive stories leaders and their congregations tell. Transition is a time of the eschatological "already not yet" expressed in the apostle Paul's vision of a new creation being birthed into our creative order (2 Cor. 5:17). The advent of a new heaven and earth (2 Peter 3:13) is both now and later, for with God there is no time, no "now" or "later." The practice of ministry in my career grew out of a commitment to the gospel expressed in the eucharistic prayers as the confession, "Christ has died, Christ is risen,

Christ is coming again." The present reality of that confession emerges as I accompany congregations in their own active dying, resurrection, and the certain hope of meeting Christ in a new emerging story of a future story.

My family member tracing stories on her son's palm was an eschatological act. In some sense she was proclaiming that the story would always be present with him, even though his hand would die by growing, shedding skin, or being covered with the calluses of labor. My realization as I write this is that my encounter with Hope was an eschatological event that redeemed the future I had not yet lived. Hope became my life center. On mornings when I feel hopeless and despondent, hope in meeting the risen Lord greets me with, "It is I, be not afraid." And that is the most powerful preface to a new story that I can imagine.

Notes

1. Kent Ira Groff, *Soul of Tomorrow's Church: Weaving Spiritual Practices in Ministry Together* (Nashville: Upper Room Books, 2000), 28–29.

2. Howard Gardner, *Leading Minds: An Anatomy of Leadership* (New York: Basic Books, 1995), 14.

3. Gil Rendle, "Telling the Story," *Congregations* (Herndon, VA: Alban Institute, 2005).

CHAPTER 7

Place-Based Narrative

PARADOXICAL LANDSCAPE
AND ROOTED REALITIES

~

SUSAN KENDALL

Every day as I come and go from the gym where I work out on Penn Avenue in Pittsburgh, I am continually startled by two elegant church spires that stand out against the sky; startled because they are decaying and fading as delicate green tiles peel and fall away, leaving gaping black squares and ragged edges. While Saint Peter's and Saint Paul's Roman Catholic Church is a designated landmark in Pittsburgh, it is now an abandoned building. There is a past: evidence of growth, of renovation, of carefully handcrafted stained glass, of an elementary school, of well-manicured lawns and well-built wrought iron fences, of carefully tended trees and flowers. All of the stained glass and windowpanes have been removed, replaced by sturdy sheets of plywood to guard against weather and unwanted entry. Latched gates that once served as welcome points are twisted and rusty. Broad and wide steps lead to solid, hand-carved wooden doors—the kind no longer made. Above the doors remains a stained glass, protected by scratched and cloudy Plexiglas, depicting grapevines and clusters of large purple grapes and designating an ascribed holy and rooted place. The text from John 15 reads: "I am the vine and you are the branches."

Pittsburgh's Search for Place

Place in one sense seems fixed, rooted. Stability equals place. In situ, one can imagine another era, another time, one in which the community and congregation were united by a common and connected community. The church's neighborhood was once a thriving gathering place in the east end of the city: active and alive. Now spray paint demarcates which gang has last claimed space and place. Wide cracks split brick from brick; the cemented mortar barely keeps the walls together. Particular scenes in the movie *Dogma* were filmed at the church in the 1990s, a story of fallen angels, with actors Ben Affleck and Chris Rock. In the movie, God appears on the church lawn. Within a five-mile radius of Saint Peter's and Saint Paul's are other spires: some small and wooden, others rounded and golden, rising higher and wider as if in holy competition, made to be visible from miles away: Pentecostal, Baptist, Presbyterian, Episcopal, Anglican, Catholic, United Methodist, Greek Orthodox, Jewish. What will be their fate over time?

Place often connotes an insider status, a known narrative, a comforting theme of shared verse, song, and memory. However, all too often the insider conversation of faith and belief becomes disconnected from the wider culture. How else are people of faith to maintain some sort of equilibrium and place of belonging? Caught in a cultural move that upends certainty, what becomes of truth, identity, community, and home, not to mention the structures that house them? Therefore, a disruptive anxiety settles upon people like mosquito netting. Fixed notions of faith and belief become counterintuitive in times of deep change. Reactions vary, but this rhythmic pattern is not a new one. It has occurred through the centuries. Place changes; the narrative shifts. Jurgen Moltmann suggests, "The founders of the modern age thought of a new, glorious era for the whole of the human race; but we are surviving on islands of prosperity planted in a sea of mass misery."[1] In the midst of endings and beginnings, churches become primary places of safety— litanies of hope, of liturgical rhythm and pattern uniting the ever-widening sacred-secular split.

Place can be perceived as static and certain and true, while actually the deeper truth shows that little of our lives and communities is static and fixed. In such uncertainty, faith—or one's understanding of it—is the first victim in at least two ways.

First, some of people of faith toss out the faith-based narrative as wrong, believing they have been misinformed about what they could depend upon, but, given what has happened, can no longer depend upon. Second, others begin to cling to faith and place as an externalized grasping for certainty and take faith and redefine it in their own terms—free from the Spirit's leading. But perhaps place can become the ground of reframing belief while keeping the tender shoots of faith growing, if we have the strength and discipline and patience. Gregory J. Riley, whose expertise in the culture and religions of the Greco-Roman world and the Ancient Near East gives him the "big view," writes that cultural change overturns beliefs—whether in the ancient world or in the present moment—thereby undermining the faith invested in them.[2] Riley, like Wilfred Cantwell Smith, whose life work was the study of the relationship between faith and belief, reminds us that *faith* is part of the human condition, while *belief* is shaped and reshaped by culture and circumstance.[3]

This essay reflects on place in relation to truth claims defined as belief, suggesting that multilayered models have always shaped our primary narratives. I believe that people of faith and their leaders, like all of humanity, live continually in an unordered multitude of voices; in the place of unending change no matter the label that contains the era and sequence of unfolding events. In the places of community where we find ourselves, pastors and leaders in the church are called systematically to be attentive to the gaps and to the disconnections that seem to appear within the narrative—both personal metanarratives and congregational narratives—so that we as leaders are able to cultivate and claim agency in the midst of change for the sake of the gospel.

Place: The Birthplace of Faith

Place becomes, then, not only a gathering site for the work of partnership, a catalyst for hope and recovery but also, many times, the very source of brokenness and loss. In the cracks and fissures, it becomes the birthplace of a deeper wisdom and grace-receiving faith.

Faith as that fundamental human yearning to connect with the transcendent is reborn again and again, rather than becoming a stagnant pool to serve as a stabilizing source and place of belonging. In a world where it is all too easy for the small, true moments to be lost to the large, place serves as a container or a containing space that gives shape to faith and to story.[4] In a strange twist of twenty-first century place, we may be told that the world is flat, boundaryless, porous, as defined by corporations and *New York Times* columnist Tom Friedman, but we the people of the world still long for community, for a place to call home, for a niche, a named and known atmosphere. "Where are you from?" is the commonly asked question. In other words, "Where is your place of belonging?"

Not a Flattened World After All

Pittsburgh is a city of hills and sharp turns, of bridges, and of a least three great rivers; a city that lends itself to poets and story. It once occupied a particular economic niche, but it has devolved to become a determined community of bridges, triangulated cityscape, and boundaried neighborhoods: Friendship, Bloomfield, Garfield, Oakland, Highland Park, Lawrenceville,

Regent Square, Homewood, Point Breeze. Tucked in the south-west corner of a perfectly rectangular state, it is neither East coast nor Midwest. Pittsburgh, Pennsylvania, is an expanse not only of churches linked by claimed sacred space and shared sacred inscription through the liturgical round from Christmas to Advent, from Rosh Hashanah to Hanukah, but also of neighborhoods, medical schools, hospitals, universities, and research centers anchored by an unchanging skyline. The primary narrative is a late nineteenth- and early twentieth-century one, except for the *religio*—the Pittsburgh Steelers, Penguins, and Pirates. An alliteration of that which binds, sports connect the community as no other thing in the city of steel. This is the only place I have preached on Super Bowl Sunday where in the first pew sat women past seventy, dressed in black and gold T-shirts proclaiming that on the seventh day God created Number Seven—at the time, quarterback Ben Roethlisberger's jersey number. I was more than instructed, I was commanded to pray in the pastoral prayer for a victory. The three major sports arenas are sacred space like no other in this city, thereby replacing the glue of a narrative of economic power and loss, of steel and glowing hot metal, with a narrative of a vital present and a hopeful future, faith in Steelers, Penguins, and Pirates.

The world we see is not flat but a terrain of variety and vistas, with the warm glow of home just around the corner. Motel 6 got it right in its advertising: a down-home, earthy voice warmly invites us to stay at Motel 6 because they will "leave the light on" for us. When do we hear that in our miniature, nuclear families? Who is willing to leave the light on for me? Pittsburgh has long held the promise of porch lights, family neighborhoods, common values and goals, good bakeries, and values of home and hearth. It still does in many ways.

Place is what informs us of identity; place provides the space for connecting what we know to be true, what we believe about ourselves, what gives impulse to live and breathe and absorb values of honesty, integrity, and faith. Place is the cradle of our identity, the nurturing parental lap that unconditionally accepts us; it is that which provides the context for the journey of self-discovery. Pittsburgh thus becomes everyone's story and search for home and place. Nostalgia gives way to the search for legacy and identity—good, bad, or indifferent.

With change comes a new search. We begin by understanding that the implications and nuances of story are patterned as they are because of place. As with faith and belief in our time, place, too, is a contested site: who belongs and who does not, and what serves as criteria for deciding? How expansive and how limiting does place become?

Place and the Narrative of Hope amidst Change

People came in waves to Pittsburgh from many places to work in the mills and factories, to produce steel and concrete, to do research, to establish corporations, and to build professions including law and medicine. They came to manage money, to engineer roads, to construct airports. They came to raise children, find stability: church, work, family, and tradition bind together a city and its people. This is a common narrative. What is different now? The world of the past was flattened, too, when ships and trails and trains served as conduits for dreams and hopes of a future. Tracing the line further, place in this corner of the globe was established first by Native Americans. What source of narrative now counts in their minds and those of later immigrants? The pattern of global realities, environmental losses, changing economic priorities, and new discoveries call into question current ideologies, presuppositions, and beliefs. In these circumstances, faith and belief often take on a stance of stability, and this is a good thing.

Place becomes the primary and first context of human actions and memories, but place as container of all contextual realities never remains the same. For us to grasp narrative as providing a common thread of identity and hope might depend on the conceptual reality that we share, first and foremost, a common dilemma. The dilemma is this—that discontinuities test the power of identity and belonging; they have tested Pittsburgh both as a memory of what might be and of what has been. Even in the midst of living *in* the narrative, there is the tension of the search for self, for testing the boundaries of ideas and roles. Pittsburgh is a city that nurtured Rachel Carson, Andy Warhol, and Annie Dillard, for example, individualists who are provocative in thought and contribution. "It was," writes Annie Dillard, "a great town to grow up in, Pittsburgh." She acknowledges that there is a "real beauty" to the old idea of living and dying where you were born. No doubt many Pittsburghers do live out this blessing. For Dillard, though, there came an urge for a new path. She was sent away to college to smooth off her rough edges. Dillard concludes, "I had hopes for my rough edges. I wanted to use them as a can opener, to cut myself a hole in the world's surface, and exit through it."[5]

Does place, therefore, allow for new frames and contexts? Yes and no. Place can hinder the new; on the other hand, someone coming to a new place may indeed experience through a new lens something connected to the old world and place.[6] What is perceived as truth and as reality, shifts with a new vista, with a new horizon, in seeing from a different angle. In the Gospel narratives when Jesus stood on the hillside, spoke from a boat in the sea, walked on the beach, paused on major highways to heal the sick and lame and blind, or proclaimed from the temple, he gave as evidence being in a particular *place*—an intentional physical presence within the venues of ordinary life. Desert, city, town, mountaintop, hillside, village, path, mud hut, tiled roof, the river Jordan: these are the places where in the intimate moments of Jesus's ministry, the Spirit brings to consciousness the ordinary and mundane of place as the primary container for human life. Such intentionality provides the concrete connection between place and person, between the mundane and the transcendent.[7] George Stroup, an early student of the importance of narrative, writes that personal identity is not the random ordering of personal history; rather, it emerges in the dialectical tension between chronicle and interpretation.[8]

Points of Connection
and Disconnection

From a postmodern perspective, we are caught in our time at the point of connection or disconnection. The depth of structural change in the world and the narrative shifts that preoccupy thinkers yield not one but a multitude of narrative interpretative accounts. Pittsburgh's sacred spaces and communities are not immune from the plentitude of arguments and perspectives and place. Like so many other sacred places and spaces, it is literally ground for splitting faith-based institutions, creed, and theology.

Place can become tragic. In the early days of the steel mills of Pittsburgh, photos reveal a world in which by noon each day, streetlights came on because of dark soot filling the skies. Mark Twain is reported to have said that Pittsburgh is hell with the lid off, as the primary light became the glow of mill fires melting steel into liquid form. At present, the steel mills and coal plants no longer provide the economic base for the city, so the air is clearer. Buildings once black as night have been cleansed, scoured with giant vats of baking soda and water—returning stone structures to soft hues of beige and gray—and revealing the solid beauty of the granite and stone. But there remains the crisis of identity: where is the soul of the city and what institutions bear responsibility for that soul?

For the human creature, place is the hope of home and of belonging. But shifting economies, the shifting earth itself, upend even this notion of security. In a globally connected world, earthquake, storms, tidal waves, forest fires, political upheaval, war, acts of terrorism, and climate change come at us like pulsing monitors recording the rhythm and pattern of a heartbeat. Where is one to be safe? Home does not protect us, even in Pittsburgh. Building on a hillside, whether for the view and vista or because it is the only available space for a shack in a crowded city, people of all means discover that the great equalizer is the pounding rain and soaked earth that gives way. In such moments compassion and pain mix together like broken and tangled lumber in a heap. What in this disruption gives solace and hope? It is the story—ours, yours, and mine—that through and in time becomes quite real in the particular moment, a narrative of faith binds up our human pain and loss. We send food and medicine and doctors and relief workers because the biblical narrative is first and foremost particular to events, circumstances. In other words, actual place becomes the string of connecting moments that sweep away false notions of God's blessing. Does this mean we are without hope as part of the narrative?

What was, as is so poignantly revealed by the silent crumbling of the historical landmark Saint Peter's and Saint Paul's, cannot be again in the same way. Each of us is shaped by the place-based narrative, and so we have a face-to-face encounter with the question: Does the narrative of any such structure contain something redeemable? Does the old giving way to the new offer something renewing rather than tragic? If so, what happens to the narrative? Any narrative is personal, but that in itself is too limiting. Place-based narratives serve to remind us of this fact. In a city with a multitude of half-empty churches and religious institutions, a recital of great events connecting place and faith reveals what happened and is happening in this place called Pittsburgh. To step back and look and see connections that formed faith and community, that continue to serve as boundaries and borders, attests to the interplay between place and story. Place, therefore, is never static; there is a fluid movement in the narrative between past, present, and future.

Place as Container of the New

Faith is neither a simple product of history nor insulated from history. Faith "is testimony anchored in history, in constant tension with it, subject to revision and understanding as well as to fluctuation in credibility due to unfolding events."[9] Place, no place, is free from unfolding events, like the floating island nation in *Gulliver's Travels* with its dirt-covered roots hanging down in anticipation of going deep into the earth somewhere, sometime. Place can become the site of an orienting experience *or* a *dis*orienting one. Going home means always going home to something different. My mother's strawberry jam on toast has remained the same wonderful comfort food for fifty years, but at some point her hands will no longer crush the berries just so, will no longer add the perfectly measured amount of sugar. It will not be the same. The jam can be made by others; the place—my mom's kitchen and the hands that make it—cannot be duplicated. Such a mundane example speaks to a larger point: the narrative informs us, gives us grounding and identity, but place can reorder what the narrative is. And to press the point further, narrative is not itself the institution. Each of us has our own distinct version of a metanarrative.

At the point of *dis*orientation, narrative of place folds into the metanarrative. Place as metanarrative becomes the containing space for the work of synthesis and integration. Opening up the grand story like butterflies from a cocoon makes visible and real a multitude of stories; all people—those of faith and those redefining or seeking faith for the first time—become connected to one another in wholly new ways through the release of our fears and dreams and hopes; through the intertwining of our pain and loss; as we forgive one another we are forgiven. Place holds the moment in time—a sequencing pattern of growth and maturity; a wisdom that allows for tension and loss and grief, while containing memories and conjuring up courage to stay alive and moving and engaged.

Do not give your heart to that which does not satisfy your heart, said the desert fathers. What has this to do with place? There comes to us at regular intervals throughout our lives a decision to live with passion and delight, to risk the deep call of God. Our stories are first and foremost internal ones and so it is that place and desire and heart connect as the creative partnership of God and human being. This is the ongoing transformation of discipline and discernment: this is the place par excellence.

Place is a defining experience for a person. Ask an immigrant from one nation to another nation, from another culture and place. Ask a newcomer to New York City or to Washington, D.C., or to Wichita, Kansas. High-rise corridors, political power, or wide open vistas shape and define each of us more than we would like to imagine. Would the church indeed have the gospel, the story of Jesus as it is, without the setting of ancient Palestine, the territory, the terrain, the weather, the culturally shaped belief and faith, the mix of tribes; without Roman rule; without a consciousness of place? Might the gospel shape Christians differently in another setting and time? Given the trajectories of certainty or uncertainty that flourish among us in our time, place replaces faith as growth and movement all too often with the unfortunate solidity of place (if I know where I am, I can know who I am). Such certainty can easily substitute for faith. This is an unnecessary displacement of primary gospel. Why? Because place-based stories are uncomplicated. All the crosses and crowns, serving as the last word atop steeples, and carvings—in addition to the chimes that echo on the hour throughout the city of Pittsburgh—are uneasy reminders that the faith-based places turn on the story of a divine human being in spite of everything.[10] Maybe this is the crux of the issue for Pittsburgh and for us all: place changes

and so do we, if we have courage to see it. We speak from where
we are as we are. Read the memoirs of Annie Dillard or Anne
Lamott. The natural flow of the divine presence permeates
each of their stories again and again. That complex problems
demand complex solutions is not necessarily true. Lamott is
transparently honest as she writes, "But I am afraid a lot, and
have no real certainty about anything." To be certain, Lamott
continues, is to miss the point entirely. "Faith," she concludes,
"is noticing the mess, the emptiness and discomfort, and letting it be there until some light returns."[11] We confuse change
with complexity.

Displaced

What is it to be displaced? Some of us are able to handle
change—we like it, thrive on it. There are those who become
clear-eyed and focused in crisis, able to guide and direct, make
lists and accomplish tasks as in no other time or circumstance.
Then there are those who cannot cope with sudden change of
place, or *any* change of place, and illness, stress, depression,
loneliness, and loss result.

I was evacuated from a flood when I was in college—out
of home and hearth—carrying one suitcase. For two or three
weeks I was displaced to sleeping in the second-floor lobby of
another dorm while my dorm was repaired. I slept next to the
soda machine—small comfort—humming intermittently all
day and night; thirsty students studying late awakened me with
the clink of the quarter, the clunk of the can dropping down for
retrieval. For years, I would not wash off a bit of mud on my
blue suitcase—I left it as a reminder of the trauma, the loss, the
unease and disruption I had faced. I am still keenly aware of
those who suffer from floods, even though my experience was
minor in comparison to many.

Something happens to the human psyche and spirit in *displacement*, particularly in sudden shifts and changes because

of trauma or loss: earthquake, fire, flood. Then there is the whole issue of displacement because of families splitting up and marriages ending, of violence and war, of moving to a new locale. Stress charts put moving at the top of what can and does cause stress.

We place our feet on the ground as we step from our homes, on the floor when we arise from a night's sleep, into the elevator to glide to our offices—we are in place step by step. This is an earthy reality. Place is always walkway, sidewalk, a path in the woods, an office or a cubicle, a seat on a plane or train. Place, in other words, becomes place only because of where we are in the moment. At one point, place *is* home, congregation, our belonging, familiarity, routine, and habit; at another, it is the change and upheaval of death and loss. How is loss tied to place? What have we lost, if anything? Does the foundation of faith crumble altogether? If I cannot place my feet on the ground as I have known—who am I?

Identity

George Stroup wrote in the early 1980s that the church and pastoral leadership are experiencing the loss of a self-consciously rooted and particular theological tradition. What is lost, according to Stroup, is identity—*not* knowing who we are as the church or as its leaders—even if we know where we are. The lament of loss is those moments of not knowing my identity, role, and function or how the circumstances at the moment are tied to Scripture and tradition.

The identity question is answered in Christian theological tradition as the place that provides the hermeneutical categories by which the community reconstructs and reinterprets its identity.[12] But, instead, that place is "an amorphous Christianity: one that is in danger of becoming unaware of its theological tradition so much so that it has begun to suffer from a form of religious and spiritual amnesia."[13] Why is this important in relation to place? Why, indeed? Because there is a cutoff, a kink in the hose of tradition, so that the sense of the vast tradition, beyond and underneath what we are the midst of experiencing, is lost.

Why, for example, do I like to go to Ocracoke Island off the North Carolina coast? I have for twenty-five years returned again and again. It is a locale of simplicity, one place that resists the accoutrements of fast food, stoplights, and boardwalk. There is silence to be had, long and quiet walks on the beach— nothing between me and the sea. Why is this important? What is at stake? For whom and why?

The pristine setting of Ocracoke Island connects me deeply with a childhood notion and experience: my country home; my grandparents' Idaho farm; my memories of the Oregon coastline where I met the Divine in storms that raged, in soft moonlight on a rare clear night, in the pulsing light of a distant lighthouse. Where might we need to acknowledge this reality in narrative form, in our theological realities of the present? The question of place is this: Why are we so easily cut off from the whole of the depth and breadth of what truly constitutes tradition? Who makes claim to tradition metaphorically and literally? This question and other wondering-out-loud moments are to guide us as Christian leaders and the church to new understandings of the narrative, connecting faith and belief to tradition.

Returning to Stroup, while he does not speak specifically of place, I offer that he assumes place as a starting point. The place in the present is what I call and what Stroup called the ambiguities and complexities of the contemporary world. It is to this wide and expansive, even overwhelming, place to which pastors and church leaders, if they understand their vocational identities, will root Christian faith with its Scripture and theological tradition. Place-based narrative is the deep connectivity of site and story. Why the resurgence of bumper-sticker theology: "Think globally, act locally"? Is place erased in a flattened and global world? Such an erasure is met with resistance. Such a metaphor betrays the creative spirit of each and every person. Such language cuts us off from the narrative of creation and gives rise to the conditions of our own alienation. Humans begin life, first and foremost, shaped and formed by place. It is a chicken-and-egg thing: the place shapes the narrative—the story—more than one might suppose. Within this interaction is the hope and promise that faith as the yearning for the Divine may be strengthened by the place of possibility, taking on new and deeper meaning for us all.

Notes

1. Jurgen Moltmann, *God for a Secular Society: The Public Relevance of Theology* (Minneapolis: Fortress Press, 1999).

2. Gregory J. Riley, *The River of God: A New History of Christian Origins* (New York: HarperCollins 2001), 231.

3. Wilfred Cantwell Smith, Faith and Belief (Princeton, NJ: Princeton University Press, 1987).

4. Dan Barry, "A Rough Script of Life, If Ever There Was One," *New York Times*, September 2, 2007.

5. Annie Dillard, *An American Childhood* (New York: Harper Perennial, 1988), 210, 243.

6. Michael Goldberg, *Theology and Narrative: A Critical Introduction* (Nashville: Abingdon, 1981), 162.

7. Sallie McFague, *Speaking in Parables: A Study in Metaphor and Theology* (Minneapolis: Fortress Press, 1975).

8. George W. Stroup, *The Promise of Narrative Theology: Recovering the Gospel for the Church* (Atlanta: John Knox Press, 1981), 124.

9. Michael Novak, *Ascent of the Mountain, Flight of the Dove: An Invitation to Religious Studies* (New York: Harper & Row, 1971), 47, quoted in Goldberg, *Theology and Narrative*, 171.

10. Barbara Brown Taylor, *Leaving Church: A Memoir of Faith* (San Francisco: Harper One, 2007), 150.

11. Anne Lamott, *Plan B: Further Thoughts on Faith* (New York: Riverhead Books, 2006), 257.

12. Stroup, 33.

13. Ibid.

Contributors

~

Robert Charles Anderson is a professional interim ministry specialist in the Presbyterian Church (USA). He has served congregations and presbyteries and is currently the interim pastor at Collingwood Presbyterian Church in Toledo, Ohio.

Judy Fentress-Williams, associate professor for Old Testament at Virginia Theological Seminary in Alexandria, is currently working on a commentary on the book of Ruth with Abingdon Press. She is particularly interested in the dialogic nature of biblical narrative and the way it invites the reader into conversation.

Larry A. Golemon is an ordained Presbyterian minister and a consultant and researcher in theological education. He coauthored *Educating Clergy: Teaching Practices and Pastoral Imagination,* the Carnegie Foundation study of seminaries, and recently directed the Narrative Leadership project for the Alban Institute and the Ecumenical Project at Virginia Theological Seminary.

Susan K. Hedahl is professor of homiletics at Gettysburg Lutheran Seminary (Pennsylvania). She researches cross-cultural modes of communication that intersect with preaching. Her published works also focus on another crucial component of narrative leadership—listening. Her teaching pedagogy consistently includes reference to the influences of culture(s) on proclamation.

Kathryn Vitalis Hoffman left her call as campus pastor and mission leadership coordinator at Gettysburg Lutheran Seminary in 2007 to serve as senior pastor of Zion Lutheran Church in Middletown, Maryland. On occasion she leads workshops and helps teach courses on narrative leadership in a postmodern culture.

Susan L. Kendall is director of the Doctor of Ministry Program and a member of the faculty at Pittsburgh Theological Seminary. She is a minister of word and sacrament in the Presbyterian Church (USA) and has served as a pastor in Washington, D.C.; Portland, Oregon; Tokyo, Japan; and Frankfurt, Germany. Currently, she is completing a book on faith in the postmodern moment, titled *Hunting for Jesus in Pittsburgh*.

Mary Clark Moschella is professor of pastoral theology and congregational care at Wesley Theological Seminary in Washington, D.C. Her recent publications include *Ethnography as a Pastoral Practice: An Introduction* (Pilgrim Press); and *Living Devotions: Reflections on Immigration, Identity, and Religious Imagination* (Pickwick Publications). Her interest in narrative leadership stems from her thirteen years as a United Church of Christ pastor.